SECRETS OF MARKETING SUCCESS

OTHER BOOKS BY LOUIS CHESKIN

SECRETS OF
MARKETING
SUCCESS

LOUIS CHESKIN

1967

TRIDENT PRESS
New York

This book is dedicated to

a searcher for new methods
to achieve success

Library of Congress Catalog Card Number: 67–16398
Published simultaneously in the United States and Canada by Trident Press, a division of Simon & Schuster, Inc., 630 Fifth Avenue, New York, N.Y. 10020.

PRINTED IN THE UNITED STATES OF AMERICA

INTRODUCTION

Louis Cheskin is recognized as America's leading motivation researcher. He has aided in the development of many outstanding marketing successes. He is a researcher who does not hesitate to make a prediction on the basis of his research. When he saw the results of the study on the 1961 Lincoln Continental, he publicly announced that the automobile would be the success story of the year and would become the car with the greatest prestige. Two of his earlier predictions in the car industry had also come true: the great success of the Thunderbird and the failure of the Edsel.

He is the author of twelve books and many articles on design, color, and marketing. His books have been translated into several foreign languages, eight of them into Japanese.

In an article in the *European Packaging Digest* (November, 1965), on the two-day seminar which Cheskin conducted in Paris on October 25 and 26, 1965, Pierre J. Louis, Director of the French Packaging Institute, wrote: "The Cheskin system of 'unconscious level testing' is widely known. The validation in the market, in sales results, of his research has placed him as the outstanding marketing research specialist. This is why forty-five executives and marketing research specialists from France, Belgium, and Holland attended the seminar, organized by the French Packaging Institute."

Following the seminars in Paris, Cheskin went to London to address British marketing executives. He discovered that

some knew almost nothing about consumer motivation research. Many thought marketing research consisted merely
of polling consumers for their opinions on various products.

The fact that consumer motivation research was conducted
with controls was new to them. Testing on an "unconscious
level" and the concept of "sensation transference" (from the
package to the product in it or from the ad to the product)
had never been introduced to London marketing and advertising circles.

During his London stay of one week, Cheskin delivered
twenty-three speeches and held five press interviews. In each
of them, audiences and the press showed great interest in the
principles of testing on an "unconscious level," the significance of "sensation transference," and the methodology of
controls.

His marketing fundamentals and marketing research principles have spread throughout Europe and are well-known in
Canada.

In his *Secrets of Marketing Success,* Cheskin tells concisely
how to succeed in marketing.

If you are in any kind of retail business or marketing, you
should study *Secrets of Marketing Success* carefully.

The ways and means leading to marketing success are
clearly presented. The bouquets and brickbats will lead you
to new ways of thinking about business problems.

You should mark this book up and follow its guidance. You
will find it highly profitable.

Louis Mariano
COLUMNIST AND ASSOCIATE EDITOR OF THE
World Book Year Book AND THE
World Book Science Year

CONTENTS

PART I

HOW YOU CAN SUCCEED

1

YOU MUST
BECOME PROBLEM-DIRECTED

THE ASSUMPTION THAT business can now be conducted like business half a century ago and the assumption that big advertising can sell anything are the twin obstacles to success.

After studying business and advertising practices for over twenty years, I state without reservations that in our highly scientific age most business is very unscientific, that is, the methods and procedures of conducting business are unscientific. The behavioral sciences are still strangers in most business offices.

In many ad agencies, specialists in the behavioral sciences are given desk space, but in most of them they are not considered vital factors in decision-making. "Creativity" is a sacred cow of the ad agencies.

Admen generally assume that mere familiarity promotes buying; they concentrate on selling to the client, not to the public. They convince the client that a large advertising appropriation for saturation advertising of the product will cause the public to buy it. Most business executives accept the agency recommendation, if they can afford it, because they believe that "hard sell" promotes great buying.

Attitudes toward a new or "improved" product are not often predetermined. When consumers' attitudes are being considered, it is assumed that what consumers say they will do, they will actually do. Most marketing research consists of polling consumers. In polling, psychological factors are

3

treated as if they were rational elements. Most present-day marketing problems are psychological. But most businessmen do not use psychological means for solving them.

What amazed me most about marketing and advertising when I entered the business field over twenty years ago was the lack of focus on problem-solving. I still find that most advertising men and many marketing men are not problem-directed; they are not primarily concerned with solving advertising or marketing problems.

Most advertising executives concentrate on pleasing clients. This fact was brought out in an article by Jack Baxter in *Advertising Age*, March 21, 1966. Baxter reported some hiring practices in ad agencies.

One man was hired as an account executive, at $25,000 per year, because he was a Yale man. The agency wanted a Yale man because the client was a Yale man.

An account executive for a cosmetics company was hired because he was employed in a television and radio manufacturing plant. Why? Because the most appreciated or valued man in the cosmetics company came from an electronics company.

Another ad agency needed a writer for a dog-food account; the agency wanted a man who operated a kennel, had been a judge at a dog show, or had written a book or a column about dogs. The agency did not ask for a man who could write advertising copy.

Of course, if the agency loses the account, the man loses the job. Baxter points out that in advertising agencies "men are hired not for their advertising ability, but for their ability to please a client."

I found that the only standard used by many corporation executives for employing an advertising manager is the number of years served with a successful company.

One of my clients asked me whether he had to pay $20,000 to $30,000 per year to have a good adman. I told him that he could get a young, top adman to start for $10,000 or less, and each year he would get a deserved increase. I designed for him a sample test, consisting of two questions about an ad, to be given to candidates for the position.

First question: "What do you have to say about this ad?"

Second question: "How can you determine whether the ad will be effective?"

Replies to first question:

Candidate 1. I like it very much.

Candidate 2. I think it is good.

Candidate 3. I don't like it.

Candidate 4. I could improve it.

Candidate 5. I think it will sell the product.

Candidate 6. It will do a selling job.

My recommendation on the basis of answers to the first question:

Don't even consider the first four men. Each one is subjective. Each stated whether he liked it or did not like it.

The only answers that are right are No. 5 and No. 6. These responses show that the men are aware that the purpose of an ad is to sell; whether they like it or not is irrelevant.

The first four respondents reveal that they are subjective individuals.

The last two individuals show that they are problem-directed; they are concerned with what they think the ad will achieve, which should be the first concern of an advertising director.

Replies to the second question:

No. 5 man: "Test the ad in a way that will show whether, after consumers read the ad, they will want to try the product."

No. 6 man: "I know good advertising when I see it. I know it will do a job."

The No. 5 man was hired. He has been very successful indeed.

Problem-directed methods like this are not common in the marketing and advertising fields. Subjectivity predominates.

Objective standards are rare both in employing personnel and in producing advertising.

The large corporations have high standards for personnel employment. But most small companies and many middle-sized business organizations lack objective standards of personnel employment for marketing and advertising positions. The men chosen to be responsible for product development, marketing strategy, and advertising policy are generally guided merely by past experience. They are unaware of changing conditions and do not know how to evaluate marketing situations. Advertising is almost completely in the subjective realm.

Therefore, if you are problem-directed, if you carry out a policy of using objective methods and follow scientific procedures, you will succeed in business.

2

FOUR PILLARS OF MARKETING

"Too often preliminary consumer tests give a product a favorable report, but when it comes to the marketplace it fails," said Harry J. Sheerin, vice president and general manager of the consumer products division of Kimberly-Clark Corporation, one of the world's largest producers of paper products. It did not occur to him that he may have had experience with the wrong kind of marketing research.

There have been many products that were successful in a test market, but failed after the products had nationwide distribution. Also, many products that did poorly in a test market gained increased acceptance when the markets were expanded.

The test market should be the final research step in launching a new or improved product. The test market does not disclose everything the marketer should know about his product.

If the product fails in the test market, the marketer does not know why. If it succeeds in that market, it does not mean that it will succeed in other markets. When you are in a test market you are revealing your plans to competition. A test market is very costly.

There are several factors in a marketing program; four are major aspects. Each of them, consisting of several elements, is a supporting pillar of the marketing program. Each element has to be tested by itself. Only one variable at a time must be tested, in order to determine its strength or weakness.

Marketing research conducted on an unconscious level can predetermine nationwide consumer reactions at a fraction of the cost of a test market, without revealing the marketing plans to competition; this kind of research shows the reasons for rejection or acceptance of each aspect of the product. If those in the consumer sample react unfavorably, the research shows why and it provides guidance for changes in the product, package, or advertising.

But an executive who has been following the same procedures for over twenty years is not out looking for new methods. To him there are no new methods. To him there is no clear road to marketing success. There is only the traditional way of conducting business, gambling, always risk.

There is actually no single road to success. At least four roads have to be taken. I have found, however, that a marketing program should be viewed as a type of structure built around four pillars and on a solid foundation.

The pillars are: (1) Product quality. (2) Packaging or styling that has psychological appeal. (3) Advertising that communicates and motivates. (4) Price that is right for the specific type of consumer—not too high, not too low.

The foundation is exposure—distribution and display.

Without this kind of marketing structure, resting on this kind of foundation, you cannot succeed in business.

Having a good product is absolutely necessary to assure business success, but it is not sufficient. Having an effective package is absolutely necessary, but not sufficient. Having a good ad agency with an effective ad campaign is absolutely necessary, but not sufficient. It is absolutely necessary for the product to be sold at the right price, but it is not sufficient.

Also, the right product, in the right package with the right advertising and the right price will not assure marketing success, if the product does not have exposure, or if it is not distributed and displayed.

First pillar—product quality has two aspects: the laboratory or specialist's standard and the consumer's standard. The two do not always agree.

It is mandatory for a new product to pass the test of the specialist and also the test of consumer acceptance. The product must have consumer acceptance on its own, without being aided by psychological devices. It must pass the consumer preference test as a product, minus brand name, without support of any kind that is not in the product itself.

Second pillar—the package must be produced to be an effective marketing tool, not a work of art or an end in itself. It must sell the product, not itself. It must convey that it contains a desirable product, not that it is a great work of art.

It must communicate graphically and semantically. It must symbolize the character or quality of the product, in design and in color, in the lettering and in the background. Both the shape and the surface convey the character of the contents and determine how the consumer reacts to the product.

The name of the product, the logo on the package—the symbolic effect of the name and the character of the style of lettering—the color and design communicate on an unconscious level and have an effect on the consumer. These are the elements that, to a large extent, determine the success or failure of a product.

Third pillar—advertising must be produced so that it motivates consumers to try the product. The advertising, like the package, has to communicate on an unconscious, as well as on a conscious, level—semantically and graphically.

Fourth pillar—the price has to fit the consumer category. If the price is too low, it is as bad as if the price is too high, because often high price is associated with high quality.

Marketing in an affluent society largely involves communication devices—in packaging and in advertising.

Packaging has to communicate and motivate consumers at the point of sale—in the supermarket.

Advertising has to communicate and motivate consumers outside of the place of sale—at home, in public places, outdoors.

To be effective, a communication must reach people both on a conscious and unconscious level. It must provide a rational basis, but it must appeal to the emotions. The emotional appeal must have the support of a rational foundation.

3

THE PACKAGE
AS A SELLING TOOL

IF YOU HAVE a good product, at least as good as competitive products, you can sell it successfully by packaging it effectively for a particular group or class of consumers.

From a practical aspect the difference in many brands is small or nonexistent, but brands differ greatly in the kind of image each presents to the particular class of consumer.

One brand may present an image of high quality and distinctiveness. An identical product may connote low quality and lack of distinctive character. The package is usually the major determining factor.

In the past, a package was a mere physical container and a measuring device. In the present market, the package is the image of the product. It is the symbol of the product. It is a communicator and motivator. Present-day consumers buy packages without knowing it.

An effective package is a selling tool; it is imbued with psychological power that is used for motivating consumers, for promoting confidence in the product or brand.

The only thing the present-day package has in common with the package of the past is that it is still a physical container in addition to being a marketing tool. Also, the present-day package must aid the consumer in using the product or in dispensing it. The present-day package must have both functional and psychological attributes.

Paradoxically, although consumers buy packages, rather

11

than products, they do not value packages; they are conscious of throwing the packages away. Consumers are not aware that they are being influenced by the package.

It is normal for men and women to consider themselves rational beings; they believe that they buy a specific brand because it is a superior product. They are not aware that it is the package that communicates to them the superiority. They are not aware of the psychological factors of the package.

To succeed, the present-day marketer must be aware that, unconsciously, consumers buy packages; consciously they buy products, that is, they think they buy products.

In many studies, we have given identical products in different packages to consumers, and invariably, from 60 to 90 percent reported that one product was superior to the other.

The package is a vital factor in present-day marketing because of "sensation transference" from the package to the product. This means that consumers attribute the effect of quality of the package to the product in the package. We very often judge a book by its cover, a person by his attire, a product by its package.

One of the greatest mistakes made in marketing is in failing to recognize that the package is a marketing tool; another common mistake is emphasizing to the consumer the importance of the package, if the package does not have a functional advantage.

The package should always play its role on an unconscious level. We must understand, if we are to be successful marketers, that the consumer will not admit even to herself that she is influenced by a package. She is convinced that she is buying a specific brand because of its quality as a product; and pointing out the merits of a package, if they are not functional factors, detracts from the product and makes the consumer feel that she is being considered a frivolous person.

We must recognize, always, that the package is a symbol of the product, a communicator about the product, and a motivator of consumers to use the product, but actually it is not the product.

The effectiveness of the package can be predetermined by measuring its objective characteristics and the subjective reactions of consumers.

The objective aspects are determined by measurements of visibility of the package as a whole, readability of the name, and eye flow over the surface of the package. These tests of involuntary reactions reveal the display effectiveness of the package.

Psychological tests are used to determine the subjective aspects—how consumers react to it; these tests reveal the kind of connotations the package has to the consumer, whether it promotes confidence in the product. All these tests must be conducted on an unconscious level, that is, without the consumers in the test being aware that the package is being tested.

Direct interviews will not reveal how the package actually affects consumers. People try to give rational answers to direct questions, or answers that are based on a frame of reference of art or design.

As marketers, we do not want to know whether the package appeals as a work of art. What we seek to find out is whether the consumers feel that the product this package contains is of superior quality, whether it is the kind of product they will buy. Only controlled motivation research can provide this type of information.

Direct questions cannot give us the true answers for two reasons:

1. The consumer is not aware that he is practicing sensation transference from the package to the product in it; he does not know that the package makes him feel that the product in it is of superior character. He (or she) cannot tell what he does not know.

2. People always want to present themselves in a favorable

light. Instead of giving true answers, they frequently give answers that are meant to make a favorable impression. Ego involvement and prestige identification promote the use of all sorts of status-seeking devices. To a direct question, people tell you that they do their buying in the finest shops, whereas, actually they may seek bargains; they tell you that they buy the finest and most expensive products, whereas, actually they economize all they can.

Because people practice sensation transference and give prestigious answers to direct questions, we must use tests that are conducted on an unconscious level. We must rely on motivation research which reveals what motivates people without the respondents realizing that they have expressed their true feelings.

The vital components of a package are the following:

1. *Brand name:* the brand name, itself, may mean the difference between success and failure. The brand name plays a major psychological role in marketing.

2. *Symbol:* the symbol or trademark plays a vital role in a marketing program. It, too, may have favorable or unfavorable connotations.

3. *Color:* the color, also, may put the brand in a favorable or unfavorable light; it may be appropriate or inappropriate for the product; it may attract or antagonize.

4. *Design:* the organization of the elements on the package may have good eye flow or poor eye flow. It may get and hold attention or fail to get and hold attention. It may have a point of focus or lack a point of focus.

Smooth eye flow and high visibility and good readability are necessary, but not sufficient. The package may be extremely attractive at the point of sale; it may be outstanding in its objective character, in attracting attention, but it may be lacking in favorable connotations. It is necessary, therefore, that the brand name, the symbol, the logo, or type of lettering and the color have favorable psychological connotations to the market or to the particular consumers.

Frequently, I recommend developing a new brand with a psychologically potent name, rather than trying to revive a dying brand name, because in our kind of society, in an affluent country, the brand name is a vital factor in marketing.

Also, the symbol or logo is a factor in marketing because it communicates the nature of the product to the unconscious mind of the consumer. A symbol or logo can communicate hardness or softness, high quality or low quality, femininity or masculinity, modernity or obsolescence, strength or weakness, delicacy or harshness; it communicates on an unconscious level, that is, people are not aware that the symbol or logo communicates all this to them.

Color is very important because it, too, reaches people on an unconscious level. A color can produce a cold or hot feeling, harsh or soft, relaxing or stimulating, masculine or feminine. It may have favorable associations with the product or unfavorable.

In predetermining the effectiveness of a package, we must test the components first, we must predetermine the psychological effectiveness of the name, the symbol, or logo; then we must predetermine the display effectiveness of the package; finally, we must predetermine the psychological effectiveness of the package in communicating, on both a conscious and unconscious level, about the product, and ascertain its power for motivating consumers to buy the brand.

One who does not fully understand the significance of sensation transference cannot conduct research for determining the effectiveness of a package as a marketing tool.

Training in art and orientation in design, no matter how great, do not provide the know-how for measuring the effectiveness of packages.

Before one can master the means for predetermining the degree of effectiveness a package has as a marketing tool, he must be able to think in psychological terms; he must have the capacity to grasp the significance and meaning of products that are characteristic of an affluent society; he must be fully aware that in our society we sell mostly psychological satisfactions, not necessities of life.

Psychological satisfactions can be sold by using psychological devices. Employment of psychological devices rests on a full grasp of the significance of sensation transference.

4

ADVERTISING
AS A SELLING TOOL

PEOPLE DO NOT REALIZE that packages are designed to promote sales; they assume that the package is a container on which there is printed matter for identification and information about the product. Package and product are one entity.

Consumers know that ads are created for only one purpose —to sell the product to them; but the average consumer is not aware that his buying a specific brand is prompted by the advertising; he generally assumes that other people are influenced by the advertising, but he buys it because he knows it is a fine product, that it is better than other brands.

A vital role of advertising is to provide a favorable climate and a pleasing environment for the brand, so that the brand name is remembered in favorable or pleasurable terms. It is the brand name that should be recalled, not the ad; the ad should be the means for promoting the brand; it should not be an end in itself.

If your brand has a good sale without advertising, advertising will increase the sale; effective widespread advertising can bring a very great sales increase.

Advertising reaches consumers outside of the store and makes possible the presentation of your product or service in the most favorable light; it provides an opportunity for emphasis, for pinpointing specific advantages.

The advertiser decides what he will and will not communicate.

In no other type of communication does the communicator have as much opportunity to be selective or is the possibility as great for promoting a specific product or service by semantic and graphic means as in advertising.

Advertising, also, is different from other types of communication in that it does not produce the effect of objectivity. It obviously is self-interested. The advertiser does not and cannot claim objectivity.

To the marketer, the great advantage of advertising is that the advertiser is master. He is free, within the law, to present his product or service in any manner he wishes.

The great advantage of a newspaper or magazine news report is that it is more believable. News is generally considered to be objective, but rarely is it as graphic, as explicit, or as pointed as advertising.

Because news is believable, PR (public relations) specialists make a contribution to business that is distinctly different from that of the advertising agency. The communications of publicists are complementary to advertising. The publicists play a major role in image-building.

The creative ad writer or artist (in advertising) can imbue a product or a service with psychological powers. If he has the ability, he can arouse interest and promote desire, semantically or graphically, but his primary purpose is to communicate and motivate, not to express himself.

His creativity must be a means for achieving the most effective communication. He must not consider the ad as an opportunity for self-expression.

Frequently, an assignment to produce an ad is considered an opportunity for creativity. Such advertising generally fails to communicate in a motivating way and is not successful in promoting sales.

Much advertising suffers from an abundance of creativity and a lack of motivating communication.

The creative aspect of advertising is basically subjective. It is the individual copywriter's contribution, the individual graphic artist's contribution. Originality and individual character are the offspring of subjectivity. Uniqueness, newness, freshness, and a stimulating effect can be achieved only by the creative person.

The subjective aspect of a communication appeals to the emotions. It stimulates interest; it creates desire. The objective aspect of the communication deals with the physical properties and functional aspects; it appeals to the rational side of the consumer.

The most effective advertising presents objective facts in a subjective manner. The objective factors or practical aspects appeal to the "logic" of the consumer, to the desire of the consumer to feel that he is practical. The subjective aspect produces an emotional response, stimulates interest, and promotes desire that is justified, by a process of rationalization, by the objective or practical aspect.

We can predetermine the effectiveness of an ad by measuring the effectiveness of the components in the ad and then testing the ad as a whole. First of all, we must ascertain the appeal or the effect of the theme.

We test four or five themes at a time.

After we have learned which of four or five possible themes is most effective in communicating the quality of the product or service, we test graphics; and finally, it is generally advisable to determine the effect of the ad or commercial as a whole.

The best presentation of a weak theme will not be effective. The best theme poorly presented will not be successful in motivating consumers.

The theme presents the concept. The graphics give form to the concept.

We use methods for testing advertising like those for testing packages. We determine how the eye flows over the ad, then we determine how the ad communicates—the kind of associations it has, favorable and/or unfavorable.

In testing an ad, as in testing a package, we talk only about the product or brand. We ask representative consumers to reveal their attitudes toward the product, as it is represented by the ad. We are not interested in the consumers' opinions of the ad, but in their attitudes toward the product in the ad.

The ad, like the package, therefore, must be kept on an unconscious level. In research, we talk about the product when testing packages and we talk about the product when testing ads.

Consciously, the consumer is interested only in the product. He does not know that the ad influences his attitude toward the product.

Fifty years ago, in a society of scarcity, the purpose of an ad was to announce the availability of a new product. In an affluent society, such as in Europe or in North America, the ad must do more than merely announce availability; now an ad must have a psychological effect, it must motivate; it has to inspire a desire for the product.

Because men and women try to give the impression that they have "good taste," are rational and practical, they say that they are interested in factual articles or literature but do not say they are interested in advertising.

Two hundred women were asked why they subscribed to a certain magazine. Over 90 percent said because they liked the articles and the cartoons; over 70 percent gave only the articles as the reason for subscribing. The study showed that over 80 percent could recall only cartoons and ads. They had not read the articles. Not even one of the 200 subscribers gave the ads as the reason or as one of the reasons for subscribing.

We have many studies showing that the effect of advertising is subliminal or on an unconscious level. Because advertising rates low in believability and is more and more limited by government regulation, it will soon develop a new character. My prediction, on the basis of some clear results of limited research, is that much advertising will take on the character of entertainment, with emphasis on humor.

5

PSYCHOLOGICAL DEVICES
IN MARKETING

THE BRAND NAME is a psychological device. The symbol is a psychological device. Styling and package are psychological devices.

Most marketing men are not fully aware how important a name is. Those who do know that it is important for a product to have the right name are not always fully aware of the psychological implications.

The chairman of the board of one large corporation did not agree with the test results that showed the name of his choice inappropriate for the product. He insisted on adopting the name of his personal choice. Millions of dollars are being spent to get this name associated with the company. The name that came out best in the test had a natural affinity to the business of the company.

The mother of the president of one of our big corporations chose the name for a product on a sentimental basis. Management had to accept it and it was a major factor in the failure of the product.

Business executives generally react subjectively to names and to graphic symbols.

The following is a record of a discussion at a committee meeting of a large company:

A. Mustang may be the best name this outfit can get. But it is not Impala.

B. *Why is Impala a better name?*
A. Because an Impala is a sleek, trim animal; a Mustang is not.
B. *Does this mean that the Impala name will sell more cars than Mustang?*
A. Impala is a better name and the styling of the Impala is, of course, superior.
B. *Why of course? How do you know it is?*
A. You can expect it to be; this company knows what car styling is.

Mr. A. appears to know all the answers. But does he? What did research show?

The research showed: Impala is the name of an animal that is "sleek" and "swift." It has factual meaning. Mustang is the name of an animal that is "rugged" and "fast." It has emotional meaning to the average American. The average American does not associate himself with an Impala; the Impala has no close meaning to him. The average American does associate himself with a Mustang; the Mustang has close meaning to him. Therefore, Mustang is a better name for a car than Impala.

Styling? The research showed that the styling of the Mustang is in harmony with the name. It rated high in association with "rugged" and "fast."

"The sleek and swift Impala is not as close to me as the rugged and fast Mustang. The Mustang is real; it is in my country and I can ride it or in it. The Impala is beautiful, but I cannot ride it; it is in a foreign land. The Impala may run away. I can control the Mustang."

These are the images of the Impala and Mustang. Research shows that these images are psychologically significant.

A study was conducted to determine which of five drawings of birds would serve best as a symbol or trademark for a product used mostly by women.

Test results:

Three of the drawings were associated with "pigeon" and the other two with "dove." Biologically, there is no difference between a pigeon and a dove, but psychologically a dove symbolizes "delicacy," "peace," and "love"; a pigeon is a "dirty bird."

Another demonstration of the significance of symbolism is revealed in a study of designs proposed for the 1967 Easter Seal sponsored by the National Society for Crippled Children and Adults. Ten design concepts were submitted for testing. They were tested in sets of five.

A seal with a crippled child (Design 2) came out considerably ahead of the other four in one set and in the other set a lily (Design 5) came out with higher ratings in favorable associations, in impact, and in preference.

The winning crippled child (Design 2) and the lily (Design 5) were put into the final test. In over-all effectiveness, the test showed, the two designs were about equal.

It is significant that Design 5 had a little wider appeal to people of the Protestant faith and Design 2 had a little wider appeal to people of the Catholic and Jewish faiths. The seals were designed by Donald Marrs.

Among the most effective commercial symbols is the Standard (American) Oil sign (an oval in red, white, and blue with a torch in the center). A series of tests during the last twenty years has shown that it is the most effective symbol in the oil industry.

In the original research, before it was known to the public, the sign rated very high in association with "oil," "American," "high quality."

After twenty years' exposure to the public, it still rates high with the same associations, and in addition, rates equally high in association with "good service," "reliability," and "helpfulness."

The original associations were inherent in the symbol. The additional associations are the result of the continuous advertising campaign and of the fact that the advertising is supported because Standard Oil stations do provide good and reliable service and the service men are helpful.

Miss Sunbeam (portrait of a little girl), the trademark of

Quality Bakers of America (QBA), is one of the most effective symbols we have ever tested.

The four-leaf clover of Good Luck margarine and the crown-in-oval symbol of Imperial margarine are among the best symbols in the supermarket.

6

VERBAL AND NONVERBAL COMMUNICATION

MOST PEOPLE ASSUME that all communication is verbal. People know that they communicate by talking or writing. But most men and women are not aware that we also communicate with symbols—images and colors.

Often, images and colors are more effective than words because people are not aware that the image and color symbols have an effect on them; they are, therefore, not defensive.

Studies of communication media—television, radio, magazines, newspapers, posters—show that images communicate more effectively than words.

To produce effective advertising for consumer products, both images and words must be used.

Words provide possibilities for image-building by the consumer which may be good or bad for your purpose.

Realistic images, illustrations of products, represent reality —the actual product. Realistic graphics are essential for showing consumer products in communication media.

But symbols and colors are more effective than realistic illustrations for producing an emotional effect on an unconscious level, because people are not conscious of the effect symbols and colors have on them.

Arrangements and designs also can be highly motivating. Few people are aware of this.

Most marketing men and many admen have little understanding of the power of nonverbal communication.

I have found few business executives who realize that non-verbal devices can be used for motivating consumers. Members of the International Consumer Credit Association were surprised to hear me say in an address at their convention on June 22, 1966, that you can motivate people to pay bills with nonverbal means.

Most people want to pay their bills. But often they have bought more than they can pay for. Sometimes unexpected emergencies cause people to spend money that was intended for paying bills.

Some bills are given a higher priority. How can you get people to give a high priority to your bills?

The usual devices are letters, reminders, warnings, etc. These means often, but not always, result in collection. But they also alienate customers.

There are nonverbal means, as well as verbal means, that can be used for motivating customers to give high priority to your bills. You can use design and color in the store, in the office, and in your mailings.

With psychologically favorable decor, you can make the customer feel that she is welcome. With psychologically potent mailings, you can make her feel that she is getting a letter from a friend.

Your customer's attitude toward you and toward your store can be "conditioned" with design and color.

A soft, cheerful environment in the credit office promotes one kind of attitude. Hard, overly ornate, "busy," harsh, and eye-fatiguing furnishings promote another kind of attitude.

Receiving a letter that is courteous and short, on dignified-looking, soft-appearing stationery reminding you that the bill is overdue is not an unpleasant experience. Such a letter is given much more consideration than a "hard-looking," glaring, cold letter demanding payment.

We must know, however, specifically, the kind of "images" and colors that produce favorable reactions and those that have an unfavorable effect.

Women react unfavorably to triangles (a triangle is a bad

trademark for a store in which most of the buying is done by women). However, both men and women react favorably to circles and ovals.

Many "hot" colors in a room are irritating. You should avoid using yellow, green, and orange in one room.

Cold colors do not promote warm feelings. You should avoid using only blues in a room.

You should combine warm and cool colors, because they are physical, physiological, and psychological pairs. They are balanced and they create a feeling of balance, which is the kind of feeling you want to create.

People cannot tell you that they are irritated by the sharp edges of the furniture or by the sharp points of your trademark, because they are not aware that it irritates them.

They look for what appear to them more rational reasons; they are most likely to blame the store, the management, the credit department.

Because of sensation transference, the irritations caused by any elements in the store or in the company are attributed to management.

Sensation transference causes people to say the food in the restaurant is not good, whereas actually, the decor is irritating; they transfer the sensation from the decor to the food.

Because of sensation transference from the package to the product in it, people buy one product instead of the competitive one—one coffee, not another, one brand of cheese, not another.

You can create an environment that promotes favorable sensation transference. You can use decor in an establishment that will project a favorable image of your company.

Also, in your mail, you can promote a favorable image with effective layout, design, and color.

These nonverbal means are effective on an unconscious level. Nonverbal means do not bring out defense mechanisms. People are not on guard against designs and colors in interiors or the design and color in letters.

Of course, the way you use words is very important. You

can make your customer feel welcome, even if she has not paid the bill that's overdue, by the way you use words, with the phrasing and with the tone of voice. This is now common knowledge. But what is not common knowledge is that you can use nonverbal means, decor, graphic devices and colors, to get customers to give your bills high priority, just as nonverbal means are used on packages and in advertising.

7

WHY

MARKETING PROGRAMS FAIL

AMONG THE PREDICTIONS of failure because of wrong package:

Food product: "This brand will fail because the new modern label communicates to consumers that the can no longer contains the original fine product. It was associated by the majority of consumers with 'artificial' and 'low quality.' "

Beverage: "This brand will suffer because the package communicates a feeling of 'not up-to-date,' 'old-fashioned,' and 'for older people.' "

The above predictions have become facts. Each of these marketing programs has failed, not because the product was of inferior quality, but because it was psychologically wrong.

A waste of millions of dollars on advertising resulted because the chief executive disregarded research and made subjective decisions:

A few years ago, one of the country's major oil companies adopted a symbol that failed every Louis Cheskin Associates test—in the gas station, on packages, and in ads. The research showed that the symbol had negative connotations. But the chief executive liked it, so it was adopted. Now, billions are spent in advertising it.

A marketing obstacle resulted because of bad marketing research:

In 1965, another oil company changed its name and

adopted a new symbol. The designers of the symbol conducted "marketing research" and they found that it had appeal. Controlled motivation research showed that it was impotent.

Business failures that were predicted by research were not always caused by weak packages or poor ads.

Women's purses: "The purses will be rejected by shoppers because the very costly 'real leather' looked 'artificial.' "

Luggage: "The luggage line will fail because it resembles a cheap line of luggage. The cheap line will fail because it appears to be heavy, yet it actually is not heavier than competitive luggage."

Men's suits: "The line of luxury men's suits will fail because the style of the suit jacket is associated more with 'refined' than with 'rugged,' more with 'leisure' than with 'business,' more with 'youthful' than with 'mature,' more with 'artificial' than with 'natural.' "

Men's coats: "The line of men's coats will fail because the manufacturer made some 'economies in details that are not important.' " (This research, unknown to the maker, showed that lack of the details downgraded the brand.)

Kitchen appliance: "This kitchen appliance will fail because psychologically it does not fit a kitchen situation; it has unfavorable associations with food."

Shampoo appliance: "This practical unit will fail because it was produced to have an image of 'luxury.' The consumers want a competitive product they consider 'practical,' 'reliable,' and 'economical.' "

The executives, brand managers, marketers are responsible for making the marketing decisions.

It is difficult for the tradition-bound businessman to accept the fact that styling or the package has to be the focal point of a marketing program and at the same time understand that the package should not be treated as a work of fine art.

It is difficult for the average marketer to realize that, in the supermarket, packages have to communicate with forms, designs, colors, and words that have desirable psychological connotations and they have to be reinforced with rational or factual information, to make the product desirable. No matter how much one is motivated irrationally, he likes to believe he has a rational basis for making choices.

Most marketing men cannot understand sensation transference; they cannot comprehend how consumers transfer the effect of the package to the product.

Equating packaging with art is the basis for many marketing weaknesses and for marketing failures.

Many marketing men have difficulty giving full recognition to the fact that the brand name is a vital part of the package, that its symbolic character has an important role which is decisive in the effectiveness of the package as a marketing tool. Brand names are usually chosen subjectively.

Package designers refuse to accept the fact that packages must motivate consumers to want the product in the package, that the package should not be wanted for its own sake, as a work of art. The designer has been educated and conditioned to think of art for art's sake. He is emotionally involved with his art.

Because the package designer is, often, one who has been trained to be a fine artist, it is natural for him to consider package design as an end in itself. A creative person is proud of his creativity. Most creative people are highly subjective and cannot consider their creations in objective terms.

There are, however, some creative people who know when to be subjective and when to be objective. Jack Roberts, who is a Canadian marketing specialist with orientation in the graphic arts, in packaging and in marketing research (he was trained in graphic arts, served as packaging director at Procter & Gamble and had research experience at Color Research Institute and Louis Cheskin Associates), has found designers in Canada who are interested in having their package designs submitted to objective marketing research. I know a few such designers in the United States, and I have found a few in Europe. Most creative people in Britain and France are just as subjective as they are in our country. Package designers and copywriters in Europe, too, want to express themselves above all else.

In packaging, and also in advertising, we deal with a paradox. The package or ad has to be original and different from any other so that it gives the brand specific identity and distinct character. At the same time, it has to communicate to large segments of consumers. It has to motivate the general public. It has to appeal to the masses.

All effective communication is the offspring of a paradox. Effective communication is not possible without creativity. At the same time, creativity is often a barrier to effective communication.

To produce effective communication one must be creative. But because one is being creative does not necessarily mean that he is producing effective communication. Creativity often is almost completely subjective in character and therefore fails to communicate or spoils the communication.

Creative people love creativity in itself. The communicative aspect is considered secondary. An assignment in communication is considered an opportunity for self-expression.

Many ads and packages fail to communicate to the great masses of people because the creative person's desire to be different defeats communication.

Subjectivity as a barrier in communication shows up in all creative expression and in all media.

Many marketers and advertisers fail to realize that all subjective expression that has to communicate should be measured in terms of communication effectiveness, not in terms of creativity or originality. Without objective measurement, the communication may turn out to be sterile because of lack of originality or subjectivity, or it may be impotent because of an overabundance of subjectivity, or too much creativity that fails to communicate.

With few exceptions, creative people detest submitting

their creations to the measure of the common denominator. They think research spoils creativity; they are not concerned with spoiling a marketing program.

Acceptance or approval by the masses is not a designer's happy dream. A prize award from a jury of noted designers or other persons of status is, however, appreciated.

How then can we be assured of getting effective communication? The answer lies in accepting the fact that creative people are subjective and should be so, but that the subjective creations must be submitted to objective measurements. This, most marketing men fail to comprehend.

Frequently, the marketer blames the creative people for failure to communicate. Putting the blame on the creative individual is a great mistake. The marketer must realize that the creative man is, by nature, subjective and that this subjectivity is the spark for creativity.

The marketer who seeks a creative person, copywriter or graphic artist, who is not subjective and is not primarily interested in creativity, is inviting failure!

An uncreative person cannot produce effective communication. For a communication to be effective, it must be original. It must have attraction-power. It must promote interest. It must stimulate. It has to motivate. To achieve effective communication, creativity is essential.

Communication without creativity is sterile. Creativity without communication is impotent.

Creativity and communication are complementary. They are interdependent. One is of no value without the other. But many admen think if you have communication you cannot have creativity.

The only way of achieving effective communication is to provide the creative person—copywriter, artist, or designer— with objective information about the problem, permit him to interpret this in his own subjective manner, and submit his creative results to the objective measurements of valid marketing research.

Most marketing men and admen do not fully understand the roles of the creative person and of the researcher.

They have not caught up with the times. They do not understand the changing social and economic conditions, from scarcity to abundance, from an economy that provides biological necessities to an economy that provides psychological satisfactions.

Advertising is a major factor in an affluent society. A society with abundance of material goods cannot function without advertising. Mass production depends on mass consumption and mass consumption is not possible without mass communication about the availability of new and improved products and also, of course, the ability and willingness of people to buy and consume them.

The new and improved products are mostly new and improved in psychological appeal, not functionally or practically. Advertising is an essential link between production and consumption. There can be no mass production without mass consumption, and there can be no mass consumption without mass communication.

Because people resist change and are suspicious of new ideas and new things, communication about the new ways of living and new products has to be of an educational and persuasive nature. Psychological devices must be used.

But, although most commodities (in fact, over 90 percent of the products in a supermarket satisfy psychological wants) are not necessities for sustaining life, most businessmen give little consideration to the psychological aspects of their products.

For example, candy has great nourishment value. However, the fact is that very few people buy candy to satisfy hunger or to give them needed energy. Actually, candy is bought because it is psychologically satisfying. It tastes good. Thus, the marketing of candy should be more in the psychological realm than in the nutritional.

Yet, most marketers of candy seem to be unaware of the psychological factors. Although they stress the ingredients in relation to taste, they disregard the other psychological factors that are involved in the marketing and consumption of candy. Most of them seem to be completely oblivious to the psychological power of design and color, and many show a complete lack of knowledge of the psychological significance of packaging.

This lack of recognition of the roles of design and color also reveals itself in candy advertising. Most candy ads are not much different in character from hardware ads.

In the last quarter of a century we have learned that various shapes have psychological connotations—some are motivating, some are not. We know that specific colors have symbolic meanings to the unconscious mind, and frequently to the conscious. Yet, the graphics that are associated with candy are decided upon haphazardly or on a purely subjective basis.

Candy of high quality is offered at high prices to consumers who can afford to pay for it, but the consumers reject it because the packaging does not symbolize the high quality of the candy. And candy intended for children, who are attracted by gaiety and the dramatic, is in packages that produce an effect of delicacy and subtlety.

Many brands of candy on the market do not have great consumer demand because they are packaged with negative symbolism—wrong imagery and wrong color. The packages are original in concept and subjective in expression; they fail to communicate symbolically and factually the character and quality of the candy.

A few candy companies are on the right track. One brand achieved great success about five years ago, after struggling with a limited market for many years. This success was attributed to many factors. The fact is that the single element that contributed most to the success of the candy was a redesigned package with a highly motivating brand symbol.

Another brand of candy had an expanding market about two years ago, mainly because the brand was endowed with a new logo that expressed the high quality of the candy.

A third candy company is having an expansion program based largely on a newly designed line of packages.

Also, a fourth candy company is increasing its business greatly by having redesigned packages with a change in the dominant color as the major contributing factor to its success.

The right symbol and an effective logo, a package with smooth eye flow and a psychologically potent color, are not, in themselves, sufficient in producing a marketing success. Distribution, display, and the other marketing factors can never be disregarded. But without the psychologically potent visual factors, the best distribution and greatest display will not result in a marketing success.

There is evidence that successful marketers do not always attribute their success to the psychological devices. They cannot accept the fact that a "minor" change in the package can be a major factor in sales.

Candy company executives were not aware of the significance of the report that showed how a closed package and window package differed in consumer acceptance. The candy in the closed package had 74 percent favorable associations and the candy in the window package had 26 percent.

The candy in the closed package had a larger number of associations than the candy in the window package with all favorable attitude terms. It rated highest with "stays fresh."

The average of price associations was 29 cents for the closed package and 28 cents for the window package. The candy in the closed package was preferred by 70 percent of the consumers and the candy in the window package by 30 percent. This test showed clearly that the closed package had more quality connotations than the window package. It also showed that the two packages could be effective in different markets, one for the "economy" market, the other for the "quality" market.

The following summarization of a study illustrates that what is generally considered a mere detail is a highly significant factor in motivating consumers:

In Test A (black and white trademarks), the Crown in open space had 82 percent favorable associations. The Crown inset had 18 percent favorable associations.

In Test B (red and gold trademarks), the Crown inset had 73 percent favorable associations. The Crown in open space had 27 percent favorable associations.

These two tests showed that the Crown in open space was effective in black and white but not in red and gold. The Crown inset was effective in red and gold but not in black and white.

The following reveals that because a label is new does not mean that it is more effective than the old label:

The milk chocolate bar with the present label was preferred by 74 percent of the children and the bar with the new red oval design by 26 percent. There was no difference in preference by age. There was little difference between the responses of boys and girls. The milk chocolate bar with the present label was recognized by 82 percent of the children.

The following shows that the shape of the candy is a vital factor:

The shapes of a brand of fruit jellies rated 17 percent in favorable associations and 16 percent in preference.

Several new shapes were tested. New shape No. 1 rated 31 percent in favorable associations and 35 percent in preference.

New shape No. 2 rated 33 percent in favorable associations and 27 percent in preference.

New shape No. 3 rated 64 percent in favorable associations and in preference.

The following shows that color of candy is a significant factor:

The color of the fruit jellies rated 37 percent in favorable associations and 25 percent in preference.

The jellies in the new color rated 61 percent in favorable associations and 60 percent in preference.

These studies show clearly that shapes and colors, design and pattern, have psychological significance and are, therefore, major factors in present-day marketing.

We now know how to determine whether the brand name has favorable connotations, whether a symbol design has favorable associations, whether a logo has good readability and also the desirable psychological connotations, whether the shape or color has appropriate symbolism and whether the marketing theme is motivating.

Those who are marketing, not biological necessities, but psychological satisfactions, such as candy, can achieve greatest success, therefore, by using psychological devices—design and color. They can predetermine the kind of design and color to use by psychological means, by using marketing research conducted on an unconscious level. This is not known to most candy company executives.

Most of them are aware that packages are vital factors in selling candy. But they do not think of the packages as psychological devices; they do not understand their true and full significance.

Marketers know from experience that the amount of display space in a store is a sales factor, but they often do not know how much of a factor. The fact that it is debated means that some marketers do not believe that it is a major factor.

A controlled study revealed that the number of brand facings is a major factor in supermarket sales.

When individual packages of a new regional brand and a national brand were exposed to consumers, the new regional brand had 62 percent preference, the national brand had 38 percent. The two packages, regional and national, were actually seen by 800 consumers in four parts of the country. In each area the preference ratings were about 60 percent for the new regional brand and 40 percent for the national brand.

When the regional product was placed in six supermarkets in which the national brand had four varieties of products, thus having about four times as much exposure, the preference for, or purchase of, the product of the national brand rose to over 70 percent and the preference for the regional product went down to about 30 percent.

The regional brand and the national brand were displayed in the stores in the following manner:

A stack of the regional brand was next to a stack of the national brand on one shelf. The shelf space was divided equally. The price was the same.

On three more shelves, in three other sections, were displayed other products of the national brand but no other product of the regional brand.

The regional brand had one-fifth of the shelf space. This meant that the shoppers had four chances in five of seeing the national brand and one chance in five of seeing the regional brand.

Also, if a shopper picks one product of a brand, she is most likely to pick the other products of the same brand. For example, if she picks a brand of bathroom tissue, the probability is very high that she will pick the same brand of facial tissue, paper napkins, and paper towels.

The regional brand rated 60 percent in preference and the national brand 40 percent when the two brands had equal exposure. When, in the store situation, the regional brand with one product had 20 percent shelf space and the national brand with four products had 80 percent shelf space, the preference for (purchase of) the regional brand dropped from 60 percent to 30 percent.

This demonstrates that display space in the store plays a major role in marketing. The package is a major factor only when it is effectively displayed in the supermarket. This is a fact every marketer must recognize in order to succeed.

Why did the business fail? Which weak link in the marketing chain was the reason for failure—was the product inferior in quality or performance? Was the styling or packaging psychologically negative? Was it priced too high or was it priced too low? Was the advertising irritating, uninteresting, not motivating? Reliable research could have prevented failure for any of the above reasons.

Blind product testing could have predetermined the degree of consumer acceptance of the product. A controlled association test, conducted on an unconscious level, could have revealed the psychological effect of the styling or package. Display tests, by means of ocular measurements, would have predetermined the degree of display effectiveness at the point of sale. The right price could have been predetermined in the same test that determined the effectiveness of the complete package. Also, an association test could have predetermined which of several marketing appeals would be most effective.

One marketer informed me that his new package that had passed LCA tests did not bring an increase in sales. He said that the new product in the line did well, but the old product in the new package did not generate new business.

After investigating the matter, it was clear that he was not conducting a marketing program. I told him that he must know the difference between "necessary" and "sufficient."

It is necessary to have an effective package in order to succeed in marketing, but it is not sufficient.

It is necessary to have a high-quality product, but it is not sufficient.

It is necessary to promote or advertise, but it is not sufficient.

It is necessary to have a sales manager who has had experience in dealing with retailers, but it is not sufficient.

It is necessary to have a marketing manager who has a knowledge of consumer products marketing, but it is not sufficient.

It is necessary to have a full line of products in the store so that the brand gets as many brand facings on display as competition, and shoppers can get all their needs in this product class of the same brand, but it is not sufficient.

All the necessary elements must be combined in the marketing process. One necessary part of the marketing structure cannot possibly be sufficient for a whole marketing program.

I spelled out all the needs. I wrote warnings and pointed out dangers. It is all on record.

Almost every one of the necessary elements of a marketing program had been disregarded.

The lack of any one of the elements listed above would have weakened the marketing program. But, in this case, all of the elements were lacking except one, the package.

Neither incentives for retailers nor advertising was used to get the packages on the store shelves.

Product quality control was not maintained.

All promotion and advertising were cut off.

The sales manager resigned because he was frustrated.

The marketing manager was discharged because he wanted to use accepted means of getting the brand into the supermarket.

A full line was never delivered to the stores. Whereas each competitive brand had package facings in four sections of the store, this brand had only one or two.

Your package and brand name are the ingredients for a successful marketing program. But the ingredients for a cake are not a cake.

The only hope for any brand is in having its marketing conducted by men with an orientation in consumer products, by men who know that neither one nor two of the necessary elements is sufficient for a marketing program, by men who know how to combine the necessary elements for successful marketing in supermarkets.

In twenty years of dealing with businessmen, I have not known a consumer product marketing situation in which there was such a lack of awareness of marketing essentials or in which so many marketing aspects were wrong.

However, as I said, ignorance of new marketing facts is common in the marketing realm. Many marketers are still unaware of the new conditions in the marketplace.

One of the greatest weaknesses in marketing, I still find, is the lack of realization that the actual sales are made in the marketplace. Often, I find an advertising program in full bloom before the packages are in the stores.

Frequently, there is an awareness that the package is a basic marketing tool, but no awareness that the effective package cannot be effective unless it is displayed. It is not yet fully understood by all marketers that a quality product can be a marketing success only if it is widely displayed in effective packages. Marketers are convinced, however, that advertising makes sales.

Most advertising executives are not much concerned about packages and display. They are almost completely involved with advertising and they put stress on creativity.

The article by Edward H. Weiss in *Printers' Ink,* "Men, Money, Machines: Building and Appraising Creative Strategy," February 14, 1964, presented a most revealing picture of subjectivity in advertising.

To this spokesman for his profession, the purpose of creativity, paid for by a marketer, is not primarily to achieve effective communication but to be creative. Ed Weiss thinks research should not be used for predetermining the effectiveness of the creativity, to learn the kind and degree of effect it will produce on potential consumers.

This well-known adman thinks that the standard for an effective ad is how "original" it is, not how motivating it is.

He does not think that originality and uniqueness are only important to the degree that they are successful in communicating to consumers and in motivating them. He fails to recognize that they are worthless, if they are ends in themselves, that they are certainly of no value to the man who wants to use them as devices for selling his product or his service.

Ed Weiss said that if you use research you become a follower, not an innovator. This is nonsense. You are an innovator when you are creating, not a follower.

The role of research is to determine which of a number of innovations will achieve the objective, or which of a proposed number of created contributions will be most effective in arousing interest, in communicating to consumers and in motivating them.

Weiss should know that creativity that fails to communicate is sterile and communication without creativity is impotent.

We must have creativity in communication, because only creative, original communication arouses interest; but we must be aware that the subjectivity of creativity is frequently a barrier in communication.

Through reliable research we determine to what degree the creativity communicates and how it communicates. This, Weiss should also know.

Research and creativity are not confusing to those who are aware that research is a measuring tool of creativity and never takes the place of creativity.

For marketers, there is a problem in differentiating between valid research and phony research—between research that measures attitudes and behavior patterns and research that reports verbalisms—between research that determines communication effectiveness and research that seeks originality and uniqueness as ends in themselves.

Ed Weiss said that, a talented and creative person needs to feel appreciated and respected. If the creative person succeeds in achieving the objective of communicating effectively, he will be made to feel appreciated and respected. If he insists on being subjective, even though he fails to achieve the purpose of his assignment, he may have a lot of fun expressing himself, but there is no reason why the client, who pays out the dollars, should appreciate or respect him.

Ed Weiss will pay "any reasonable amount to get people with talent." Who will determine whether the talent is purely bravado or effective communication—whether the talent is purely personal expression or motivating communication? Valid research can determine this, not the creative person himself and not "research" that is controlled by the creative person.

He says, "Advertising basically deals in intangibles, because it involves people more than things. It involves faith, trust, confidence, style, flair, intuition, and the secret places of the heart much more than the cool recesses of the mind." The scientific process, that is, scientifically controlled research, determines whether the communication promotes faith, engenders trust, inspires confidence, expresses style, contains flair, touches the intuition, and reaches the secret places of the heart and the cool recesses of the mind.

We must use measuring devices for determining the exact nature of the creativity and its effect.

The problem-directed marketer seeks highly creative persons because he knows that creativity is essential in communicating effectively, in arousing interest, and in promoting desire. He also knows that neither he nor the creative person can possibly determine which of a number of communications—themes or designs—will be most effective. He knows that it is not possible for him to eliminate his subjectivity and that he could not react in the same way that the majority of potential consumers would react.

He knows that making judges out of consumers is not research, testing memorability of ads does not produce valuable information, asking direct questions does not provide true answers.

The problem-directed marketer knows that people practice sensation transference, that they judge a book by its cover and a product by its package and its advertising. He wants research to determine how effective the advertising (also the package) is in selling his product, not how original it is.

Up-to-date marketers know that communication effectiveness can be measured; marketing themes and ads can be measured and are being measured.

But most admen do not accept the fact that advertising must stress communication, not creativity, that communicators must deal with semantic meanings, not with meaningless words, with graphic images, not meaningless graphics.

Advertising must become an integral part of the marketing program and each of the components of the marketing program must be put to validated research. But it is not widely known that only thus can marketing success be assured.

Many admen still insist that by advertising they can sell anything in any market. They fail to accept the fact that well-conceived advertising can only be successful in selling a product of quality; it cannot succeed with an inferior product.

The marketplace is full of examples of marketing failure because the product lacked quality, or because the public had no confidence in it.

A popular brand of seafood lost almost all its customers when news broke that two died from eating it.

A Detroit automaker launched a car (the Edsel) with an advertising budget larger than any car ever had. But the people did not buy it, and it became the greatest failure in automotive history.

Up-to-date marketers know that in a highly competitive market, the product must be designed to fit the consumer. Whether a specific product meets the needs and will satisfy the wants of the potential consumers can be determined through marketing research.

But some advertising men will undertake to sell anything. They are convinced advertising is the cure-all, that it is the remedy for all marketing ills.

If sales are low, you need to increase the advertising budget, say these admen. They do not look into the quality of the product; they do not evaluate the packaging (the visual manifestation of the product); they do not make a study of the price in relation to the socio-economic condition of the consumer; they do not consider ads that will bring out the real benefits of the product; they become involved with advertising creativity. They concentrate on unusual effects and on designs to stimulate the imagination.

Because marketing executives and admen are subjective, millions of dollars are invested in ineffective packaging and impotent advertising.

An advertising executive thought that a home furnishings ad showed great graphic originality. Research showed that it rated 91 percent in favorable associations. It had great appeal indeed. But 94 percent of those who saw the ad did not know what it was selling. It failed in its objective. This was a clear case in which subjectivity (of the creative man) became a barrier in communication.

A home appliance ad contained "interesting" copy consisting of over 500 words. Research with a sample of potential customers showed that 93 out of 100 who saw the ad did not read the copy. Of those who read it, only two considered buying.

Sales indicated that a marketing theme for a food product, chosen on the basis of subjectivity, had been alienating consumers during the two years it was on the air. Another marketing theme, created at the same time by the agency, but not used, rated high in Louis Cheskin Associates research. When it replaced the old theme, sales increased almost immediately.

Many reasons were given for the failure of a line of cosmetics. The ad agency was blamed, and competitive brands were given credit for keeping it from achieving success. Research showed that the weakest link in the marketing chain was the logo on the package. It had been chosen by the top executive. He was a large and forceful man and he liked big, solid, heavy letters. The executive's subjectivity was a great barrier in communicating the high quality of the cosmetics. The logo communicated the strength, weight, and forcefulness of the executive, not the delicacy, femininity, and fine quality of the product.

The officers of a company coined a name for a new product that incorporated part of the company name and the word that described the process of producing the product. Research showed that the name had no meaning to potential buyers, though it was a meaningful name to the management and to the technical men. The subjectivity had become a barrier in communicating to consumers and an obstacle in marketing.

A problem-solving marketer has to think about the consumer, his customer. A problem-solving businessman sometimes uses the pronoun "I." He says, I found out; I learned; I delivered; I collected; I expanded, etc.

The designer, however, usually considers the "I" on a purely subjective level. He says, I love; I have; I did it.

Says designer Morton Goldsholl: "I abhor being told by motivational researchers how people feel. The artist or designer has only to look inside himself to see what is acceptable in terms of color and so forth. I'm a painter, it's part of my training. Research cuts off progress and change."

It should be kept in mind that this man is producing communication tools—packages that are intended to sell goods to the public. Those who pay for his creations are interested in attracting ordinary consumers. This designer says he "has only to look inside himself to see what is acceptable." He is expressing the attitudes of most designers. This kind of attitude is one reason why there are so many marketing failures.

The major reason for business failures is, of course, that the marketing executives approve of this attitude. They do not understand the role of sensation transference. They are concerned with status, with who does it, not with how the marketing problem can be solved. They ask, is he a famous designer, not, can he produce marketing tools. They thus become spoilers of marketing programs.

Frequently, marketing executives fail to realize that although people behave irrationally, they like to think that they are rational.

The fact that a grocery product was put into a new package was advertised on television and in magazines. The marketer and ad agency operated on the assumption that consumers are interested in packages. Since effective packages increase sales, they reasoned, the advertising of the packages should bring even greater sales. They did not know that consumers are unconsciously affected by packages, but they are consciously interested only in the product.

The marketing man who announced his product was available in a new package intended to communicate that the product was now more desirable. But he actually communicated that money was spent on dressing up the same old product. In effect, he was asking consumers to pay the cost of dressing it up.

He would have been successful in his communication if he had advertised an improved product and had shown it in a new package. The advertiser should show the new package and talk about or write about the quality of the product.

Although consumers' buying practices are irrational, people must have a rational reason for buying. This, many executives fail to realize.

A woman keeps on buying rich cake because she enjoys it. But she will buy it much more frequently if she can have "evidence" that it is good for her.

She buys a dress because she likes it. But to rid herself of guilt feelings, she justifies the purchase with rationalizations such as needing it for her husband's office party or for her daughter's school reception.

In our affluent society, the wife of a senior executive or successful professional man buys a fur coat for over $3,000 and immediately begins to economize on groceries to make up for the extravagance. She often saves as much as $3 by buying less costly meat, bread, and coffee during the period she is dominated by the guilt feelings, usually about two weeks.

Practical or rational and impractical or emotional factors are involved in the purchase of a product. A marketer who does not know this invites failure.

Many assumptions about marketing are fallacious.

IN BRIEF, THE FOLLOWING ARE EIGHT WAYS THAT
ARE SURE TO LEAD TO MARKETING FAILURE:

1. Proceed on the basis that all you need is a good product and it will sell itself.

2. Operate on the basis that a big advertising campaign can sell anything.

3. Proceed on the basis that effective ads have to be "creative" above all else.

4. Operate on the basis that a new package is a cure-all for sagging sales.

5. Proceed on the basis that consumers love new, modern, highly "original" packages.

6. Operate on the basis that "marketing research," in which people are asked to tell you which of a number of packages or ads they like, is a reliable marketing guide.

7. Proceed on the basis that "creative" advertising or "modern" packages are a substitute for a high-grade product.

8. Operate on the assumption that the "expert's" professional or management concept of quality is also the consumer's concept.

8

SUBJECTIVITY
LEADS TO FAILURE

THE EGO IS A VITAL FORCE. It is a basic factor in achievement, if it is associated with problem-solving. The ego plays a constructive role only if it is problem-directed. To succeed, one must get ego satisfaction in problem-solving.

Most businessmen, however, are subjective. Business decisions are generally made on a subjective basis. Subjectivity leads to failure.

In our highly scientific society with its greatly developed technology, many marketing executives know little or nothing about measuring consumer attitudes or they disregard marketing research primarily because they have been conditioned to make decisions on a subjective basis.

Also, most admen who serve the marketing executives are opposed to communication research because they consider creativity or originality as the essence of advertising and research as a limitation on creativity.

Subjectivity is a great obstacle. You can be sure to succeed only if you eliminate this obstacle and keep an objective position.

Few executives are aware that their decisions are subjective. Most executives assume that their choices are rational, that their judgments are made on the basis of objective facts.

Each person has an individual sense of values that he begins developing on the day he gains the power of perception, when he is only a few weeks old. A person's total personality is, in part, inherited; most of his characteristics or his behavior patterns are acquired from his parents, teachers, neighbors, other members of the community, and from the communications media.

The values one has are not only individual; they are also the values of the social group to which the individual belongs —the community, socio-economic class, nationality, etc.

A few individuals do not follow the behavior patterns of their group; they discard the influences of their early years. This often happens because of a traumatic experience or because of a startling discovery, which may be called a revelation.

Let this book be your discovery. In order to free yourself from a frame of reference that has no value in present-day marketing, you must analyze men in business and also analyze yourself. You must study the behavior patterns of executives. You will find that most men follow a single track.

You will be closer to success if you are flexible; you must not follow one road; you must feel free to react to new situations and to people—all kinds of people—to consumers and to men in competition.

In the business realm, an executive who has risen from the production phase of the corporation or business usually continues to make all decisions on the basis of his production or shop orientation.

The executive who had his business beginnings in sales generally continues to think of the entire business only, or almost entirely, in terms of sales procedures and strategy.

An executive who rose from the ranks of advertising is most likely to draw conclusions that advertising is the major factor in marketing and is the only basis on which a company can operate successfully.

Executives who enter a particular business as investment experts almost always think only of acquiring new properties.

Then there are research and development-oriented people who have their kind of values.

There are even individuals in corporations with almost purely "social service" values—as "the primary purpose of this publishing house is to raise the intellectual level of the people; we must make a profit so that we can achieve our objective in the best and quickest way."

To succeed in business, you must always be aware that the success of a company producing consumer goods depends on the consumers' attitude toward the goods and the degree of acceptance of the commodity.

It sometimes happens that the desire, taste, or opinion of the decision-making executive coincides with the desires, taste, and opinions of the public. But a marketing program cannot be based on such possible coincidence.

The purpose of business is to earn a profit. But, although business is supposedly conducted with the profit motive as the sole basis, actually, personal values often override the profit motive. For example: the Edsel name was not chosen for the new car on the basis of evidence that it was the best name for a car, because it would motivate the greatest number of buyers.

Management had evidence that the name Mustang would sell more Ford cars than any other name; Edsel was chosen only for sentimental reasons.

The styling of the Edsel was also chosen because it appealed to management. There was research evidence that the styling of the Mustang would appeal to young people, just as the name Mustang would appeal to them.

Subjectivity in decision-making is found in many, if not most, corporations. Subjectivity in decision-making is traditional. In a society of scarcity, the needs for success were individual initiative, enterprise, and stamina. There was a ready market for new commodities.

Now, we sell mostly psychological appeals, not necessities for daily life.

Your personal attitude toward a product may not at all be

like the attitudes of the great number of consumers. Present-day marketing involves many psychological problems; consumer behavior patterns in relation to the product must be predetermined; consumer attitudes must be ascertained before launching a new product.

To assure success, you must never assume, as many executives do, that because something—product, package, ad campaign, etc.—appeals to you, it will appeal to the public.

I am amazed to find researchers operating on the assumption that men and women can tell why they want a specific article.

Just as amazing to me is the fact that there are executives in the automotive industry who assume that they are able, and believe that they should be able, to determine what will appeal or will not appeal to the average person.

Still more amazing is that intelligent people equate memorability with appeal, visibility with preference, and hard-sell with great demand.

I have come across many fallacies in my twenty years' contact with business. I have encountered executives who equate a wish with a fact. I have frequently seen men in responsible positions lacking the ability to discard old methods and procedures, men who could not change their frames of reference. I have witnessed much semantic confusion.

Two opposite views came to my attention when I began to investigate the marketing of automobiles—one, that you can predict consumer attitudes toward car styling by asking people; the other, that you cannot predict car-buyer demand because the taste changes before the car is out on the market, being about three years in the design and development process.

Our studies show, and studies conducted by others have shown, that both views are sheer nonsense.

There is unquestionable evidence that people cannot tell why they make choices.

Also, there is just as much evidence that men and women normally cling to the old, that taste does not change, unless there are social pressures to change it. Although the Lincoln Continental retained its basic (1961) styling for five years, it continued to be in demand.

The belief held by many marketing and advertising men that the purchase of a costly article is primarily motivated by promotion and advertising is a fallacy. This was demonstrated by the failure of the Edsel, the most promoted car.

Many marketing men have failed to realize that the Sputniks, the international, political, and economic changes have had a great effect on marketing.

Compact cars are everywhere; the gaudy trim has disappeared from cars, but most businessmen cannot understand why we have had these changes. They do not see the connection between psychosocial or socio-economic changes and changes in public taste. They merely assume that people want to see a change every year, even if it is not a change for the better.

There are some executives who are aware that their standards are different from those of the general public or from most of the consumers of their products; at least they think the taste of the public is not as highly developed as their own tastes. Executives often have doubts about the price— whether consumers can afford to pay, or will pay, the set price for a certain article; they, therefore, seek information from representative consumers.

They become frustrated, however, when they find, which is often, that the behavior of the consumers does not match what the consumers said they would do. For this reason, executives come to the conclusion that there is no way of finding out what people really want—what people will actually buy —and, therefore, they decide that they might as well make decisions on the basis of personal opinion. They take chances; they risk the investment on a product they personally "think" is good. This you must never do, if you want to be sure to succeed.

Subjective decision-making is common in the advertising field. This is the area in which millions of dollars are wasted because advertising is produced to please an executive.

Because advertising involves great sums of money, it is implicated with a socio-economic power structure and engenders much waste in effort, time, and money. Because it is entrenched, its mistakes are perpetuated.

One major weakness in advertising is that the ad agency receives a 15 percent commission on money spent, not on amount of work, on quality, or on achievement. The size of the reward is based merely on the amount of spending.

A few leaders in the advertising field have taken the initiative to break the 15 percent formula. Outstanding among these leaders is David Ogilvy. To marketing men, it is not news that David Ogilvy is a highly successful adman.

David Ogilvy says: "A good advertisement is one which sells the product without drawing attention to itself. It should rivet the reader's attention on the product. Instead of saying 'What a clever advertisement,' the reader says, 'I never knew that before. I must try this product.'" And Ogilvy states: "It is the professional duty of the advertising agent to conceal his artifice."

He is saying that the effect has to be on an unconscious level, that the creative, semantic and graphic devices should not be ends in themselves, but should be means of engendering interest in the product by directing attention to the product and by motivating the consumer to want to try the product.

Marketing men should know that this kind of advertising is the only kind of effective advertising; all other kinds are mostly a waste.

Rosser Reeves, another top-notch adman, agrees with Ogilvy. He, too, made a great success in advertising because he understood the psychological fundamentals; he knew how to produce motivating communications and how to implement them.

We must keep in mind, however, that advertising is only one pillar of a marketing program.

Although Ogilvy is without doubt one of the most capable admen, he does not see a marketing program as a whole.

In his book *Confessions of an Advertising Man* (Atheneum) he says he seeks accounts that meet ten criteria:

"The product must be one which we would be proud to advertise. On those few occasions when we have advertised products which we privately despised, we have failed."

Note the subjectivity. He cannot be proud to advertise a product he does not like personally. The product he likes is, in his mind, the product the public will buy.

Ogilvy knows that creativity is a means, not an end in itself. He has demonstrated that he is a master in producing motivating communication.

But he implies that he sees nothing of importance between the advertising and the product he wants to sell and thinks he can sell. His first criterion is that he personally likes it and is proud of advertising it.

In his book, David Ogilvy reveals that he is an advertising man with great skill; he lists his achievements. He indicates that he has no knowledge of, nor interest in, the total marketing problem that a producer and distributor of consumer goods has.

What is more, he treats the readers of his book as he does the mass consumers in his ads; he reports what he has achieved, what he likes and does not like. He does not explain the principles that are the basis for his achievement.

We get from Ogilvy's book a number of false impressions.

When he says he believes in using research, very much research, the implication in the book is that he means polling or getting consumers' "opinions." He conveys this by repeating the name of Dr. George Gallup, the well-known opinion pollster.

He produces the impression that advertising, that is, the right kind of advertising, is the only essential for successful selling of consumer goods. In his book he assigns no great importance to the package; he does not even list it as one of the essentials in marketing consumer products.

Having worked with his agency on several projects, I know that he does not consider polling reliable research. He knows that research has to be conducted on an unconscious level, just as advertising has to be effective on an unconscious level. That is why he wanted me to conduct his research and asked me to work closely with his research people.

Also, he knows that the package is a vital element in a marketing program. He did not proceed with an ad campaign until he had evidence that the package was right in display and in psychological connotations.

His subjectivity, I think, is mainly an effect. Also, I know, he seeks objective information about the quality of the product. He insists on high quality.

But, David Ogilvy does not provide guidance on how to succeed in business, or even how to succeed in advertising. The title of his book could or should have been *I Succeeded in Advertising.*

Many marketing programs fail because there is a void or great weakness between the product and the advertising. The too common assumption is that you need a product, a great sum of money for advertising, and a smart adman. With this combination, some believe, success is assured. The evidence is that this is the road to failure. Occasionally, by sheer coincidence, a new or improved product, conceived and produced on a subjective basis, happens to fill a need or want of a large segment of consumers. The probability for this to happen, however, is very low.

In problem-solving, one must not assume that he has all the

information related to the problem. Those who insist on solving problems on the basis of their own frame of reference, or on the basis of their subjective reactions, usually become failures. Under present conditions most problems are complex. An individual's experience or knowledge is not a reliable basis for decision-making, as is shown in the following example.

A gentleman from India proposed that I establish a motivation research service in India. I told him that motivation research plays a vital role in an affluent society; it is a factor in determining the kind of psychologically meaningful products that will have greatest appeal and acceptance. I did not see, I said, how motivation research could be of any value in India —a society in which 90 percent of the people have to struggle to earn enough to maintain life.

"You are right that only 10 percent of the people in India are affluent, but I want to call your attention to the fact that the 10 percent are 40 million people," my visitor from India reminded me. This is a much larger number of people than in any one of the affluent countries of Europe.

From a business aspect, there is a difference between those who are affluent in India and those who are affluent in the countries of Europe. In India the wealthy are dispersed over the entire subcontinent. The European countries are relatively small geographic areas with highly developed transportation and communication systems. Nevertheless, India does have a large affluent sector and does consume luxury products.

My focusing on the great mass of the Indian poor blinded me to the fact that there are also 40 million who are well-to-do. This shows how easy it is to make a decision on the basis of the wrong frame of reference. I know that I have to watch myself.

Many people do not think they have to watch themselves. They are suspicious of others, not of themselves. "What is good for me or for my company is good for the country," said one of our leaders.

Most business executives sit in their offices and assume they know what the average consumer will or will not buy. (Many of our government officials and legislators also assume that they are observing actual conditions in a foreign country at war when they are on a conducted tour. Their conclusions are based on brief observations of a very complex situation.)

The subjective person is often a spoiler but he is not aware that he is; he gives no recognition to the possibility of his being one. He does not doubt his frame of reference; he does not believe he is being subjective. His doubts are only about the intentions and ways of others.

Some marketers, in spite of twenty years of validated marketing research conducted on an unconscious level, choose the kind of research that is of no value in solving business problems. In fact, it is research that may lead a businessman to ruin. He chooses this kind of research because it fits his frame of reference. It appeals to him because it fits his "thinking" pattern.

On June 2, 1965, the *Wall Street Journal* featured an article with the headline, "More Firms Go Directly to the Public For Aid in Designing Products." Obviously, the *Wall Street Journal* would not have had the article if it did not think that the readers, mostly business executives, did not need and want this information.

According to this article, up-to-date firms go to consumers for guidance on what they will or will not buy. The assumption is that consumers can and will tell what they like and want. Ronald G. Shafer, the writer of the article, obviously did not know that there have been many marketing failures because firms followed what consumers told their researchers. The writer showed no knowledge of motivation research and no awareness of the pitfalls of responses prompted by sensation transference and by status-seeking.

An example of marketing research was a statement by a mailman who said: "I'd prefer to use tissues, but they're too small and I blow right through them. What I need is something big and hefty, something suitable for a man." This and similar statements were major factors in Kimberly-Clark's decision to bring out its "Man-Size" Kleenex, said the writer. He did not seem to know that a banker, insurance man, teacher, or preacher—might not feel free to state that his nose is filled with mucus, that the blows from his nose are hefty and he needs a hefty tissue.

"Kimberly-Clark's careful attention to the views of consumers exemplifies a current trend in market research," stated the writer.

(But I stay in business because I have demonstrated that paying attention to what consumers say is an invitation to failure, that generally consumers do not know why they prefer one brand over another and if they do know, they frequently do not want to tell you.)

The writer reported: "Consumers are supplied with samples of products for appraisal and testing." He didn't explain the difference between blind product-testing and the testing of psychological factors.

In a blind product test, the consumer is given two products that differ in some properties, but neither of which has a brand name or design. This test is conducted to determine which of two products, without the support of psychological elements, has the acceptance of the greater number of consumers. This test is valid because psychological factors are not involved. There can be no respondents' ego involvement and no sensation transference to the product from the package design or brand name. The product is on its own.

But as soon as there is a name, a design, or a package, the consumer's advice is worthless, because he reacts to the package and believes he is reacting to the product.

Shafer also reported: "Advice from consumers isn't always

good." He cited an example: Bulova Watch Company was given consumer study results that indicated consumers generally seemed to have little or no interest in precise accuracy. Bulova ignored the research results. "Today the Accutron is the best-selling men's timepiece in the $125 and up category," said Alexander D. Goodman, the company's director of marketing research.

In blind product-testing, where psychological factors are not involved, the respondent feels he is rational in saying that he likes one product better than another. The Bulova problem is in the psychological realm. A man who is asked whether he is interested in his watch having precise accuracy may not say that he is, because of an unconscious fear that he would appear petty and unrealistic. To get the right answer to this problem requires testing on an unconscious level.

Only motivation research with its indirect testing methods can be sure to get correct answers to such questions. Obviously, this kind of research was not used by the Bulova Watch Company.

The *Wall Street Journal* article contained further evidence of a lack of awareness of psychological factors. Shafer reported what he was told by business executives. And what he was told revealed an abysmal lack of scientific marketing. It disclosed that a majority of marketing executives cannot differentiate between reliable and unreliable marketing research, because they are unaware of the difference between rational and psychological factors.

William Bernbach, president of the ad agency, Doyle, Dane and Bernbach, stated: "Research tends to perpetuate mediocrity because it is based on what has gone before—nothing fresh." This was reported in the *Wall Street Journal*, August 12, 1965. He said that the "We Try Harder" ads for Avis did not come out favorably when they were tested with "some car-rental customers."

The customers were asked how they liked the ad or

whether they liked it. The rational answer is, of course, that they do not like a No. 2 service; they want the No. 1 service. This is the rational answer to a pollster's question.

Kimberly-Clark management may have derived the right information by asking consumers some direct questions about a new product. I have been told that this company has had experience also with wrong answers to direct questions of their researchers.

Bulova management was fortunate in that it disregarded the answers given to the pollsters about the Accutron. They gambled and won. (The Accutron is actually a completely new, revolutionary product with psychological appeal, as well as greater efficiency as a timekeeping instrument.)

Bernbach disregarded the "research" that revealed how people reacted to the Avis ad, not how they reacted to the service offered in the ad, and produced a successful ad campaign. (That was fortunate, but I know his agency has also disregarded disclosures of reliable and valid research.) The question that had to be answered was whether the "We're only No. 2—We try harder" motivated people to rent cars. But the information that I have about the research reveals that the question put to the car renters was whether they liked the ad.

When an advertising "genius" or marketing "genius" shows that his judgment is superior to research, it is always to "bad research"—polling, direct interviewing, the kind of research that reveals verbalisms of consumers, not their behavior, research that records responses, but does not disclose attitudes.

The pollsters keep right on asking questions and getting answers that have no relationship to actual behavior. Polling continues, although for many years the behavioral sciences, and LCA marketing research for over twenty years, have been demonstrating that men and women cannot tell how they feel about anything that has psychological, not rational meaning.

Polling is acceptable because it is familiar; it has been

around for a long time and it is in keeping with the education we received. We learned that you get answers by asking questions. Questions and answers are basic in the educational system of a society of scarcity, a society in which psychological aspects were not major factors in daily life.

Most management men either rely on the answers given to the pollsters, thus inviting disaster, or they disregard marketing research, make decisions on a subjective basis, and gamble with great investments. Subjective decision-making is traditional. Businessmen have "always" made decisions subjectively. The "shrewd" ones made correct decisions and the others made wrong decisions. This is the traditional concept of decision-making in business.

Package designers and the graphic artists in ad agencies have been educated in art schools, where self-expression is stressed. Originality is the essence of "modern" art. Subjectivity is glorified in contemporary art circles.

Marketing would not suffer from the subjectivity of creative people—graphic artists, copywriters, and package designers—if marketing executives were not subjective.

But, most marketers do not understand the psychological implications and do not believe that the effectiveness of packages and ads can be predetermined, because they have not been conditioned to deal with psychological problems.

They are accustomed to thinking of the package as a mere container and of advertising either as a mere announcement or as an attraction, more akin to entertainment than to motivating communication. The concept of sensation transference is foreign to them. Ego involvements in answers to direct questions are not recognized by them. Subjectivity prevails. This subjectivity leads to failure.

9

RESEARCH
THAT LEADS TO FAILURE

MUCH OF WHAT IS CALLED RESEARCH is actually non-research posing as research. Non-research is commonly used for making subjectivity appear as objectivity; it often serves as a means of presenting personal opinion as the objective reporting of fact.

For example, on January 26, 1967, the *Wall Street Journal* had an article with the headline "Not Buckling Down: Most Motorists Shun 'Ugly, Cold' Seat Belts." Evidence was presented that most motorists do not like seat belts: "one woman recently took off her shoe, and used the spiked heel to smash part of the instrument panel on her 1966 Thunderbird. She wanted to extinguish permanently the reminder light that glows until the driver buckles up." It was pointed out in the article that on the 1967 T-birds, the light goes off after ten seconds, whether the belt is buckled or not. The implication was that the change in the 1967 model to a mere ten seconds' warning was made on the basis of this evidence.

More evidence was presented that people do not like seat belts: "A construction worker in Detroit took delivery of his new car and then carefully snipped off the belts when he got home." An office worker in Detroit said "they give me cramps"; a switchboard operator did not use seat belts because "they rumple your dress." A man said he had three accidents and each time he was saved because he was thrown out of his car.

In addition, the conclusions of a well-known motivational researcher and his evidence were presented. One young teacher told the researchers: "On a date I'd take the man without a seat belt. There is something sort of homely, stodgy and cowardly about these belts!" For a young housewife, seat belts recalled ugly childhood memories: "Well, it's like sitting on a toilet, being strapped down to the toilet."

Tim Metz, writer of the article, presented the outbursts of fewer than a dozen individuals as evidence and the motivational researcher provided a consumer sample of two.

Millions of car drivers are concerned with seat belts, yet the writer considered a few eccentrics and neurotics as representative of American car owners.

This and other articles written on the basis of non-research posing as research are read by business leaders, who often make decisions on the basis of such articles. After reading this article, many are of the opinion that car owners do not like seat belts.

Actual research shows that most drivers are still not used to seat belts and many are not convinced that seat belts are truly a safety factor. In time, car owners will get used to seat belts and an education and information program is needed to make car owners aware that, when used, seat belts save lives. At the end of the article, the writer does state that the American Seat Belt Council, an organization of belt makers, is producing filmstrips for television, showing unbelted dummies being thrown through the windshield in collisions. Unfortunately, most of the readers read only the headline or only the first two or three paragraphs. They only learned that most people do not like seat belts.

Non-research, the kind of research in which a few individuals, often eccentrics and neurotics, are considered a sample of consumers, is popular in some marketing circles.

There is another kind of non-research that has even wider acceptance. It is research in which interviews are conducted on the assumption that men and women can and will give

true answers to all questions. Defense mechanisms—ego involvement and status seeking—are not recognized; sensation
transference is unknown. This kind of non-research im-
presses many with its precise socio-economic sampling or with
large numbers, many hundreds of interviews. The "researchers" are not aware that the responses are not the true attitudes
or real feelings of the carefully chosen consumers, because the
respondent either wants to make a favorable impression on
the interviewer or cannot give the right answer because of
sensation transference—the respondent transfers the sensation from the package to the contents; he judges a book by its
cover.

Both kinds of non-research lead to marketing failures.

To be effective, advertising must communicate *and* motivate, not merely communicate. The package also must communicate and motivate. Some marketing researchers know
this.

But even these researchers are often spoilers of marketing
programs because they try to use research methods that are
effective in other fields, not in business.

"Must Advertising Communicate to Sell?" was the title of
an article in one of our finest business magazines. The author
used several hundred words to explain that communication is
not enough, that an effective ad must do more than communicate—it must sell, and that testing the effectiveness of advertising is complex and costly. He should have added that
the methodology he described is not reliable.

This article did not convince the marketing men who read
it that marketing research—pre-testing of advertising—is economical and a reliable guide in making marketing decisions.

Marketing research suffers from overspecialization. Some
marketing researchers are deeply concerned with the consumer's psyche. Others concentrate on numbers; to them the
more people they can count, the more reliable the information they think they have. Still others are absorbed in social
classes; they are completely involved in the sociological aspect

and they disregard all other aspects. All three—the psychoanalytically, statistically, and sociologically oriented researchers —do not use research controls to prevent ego involvements and defense mechanisms entering the research situation and show no evidence that they are aware of sensation transference, that consumers judge a product by its package and a book by its cover.

Researchers who were trained as statisticians concentrate on producing elaborate statistical charts of respondents' verbalisms on the assumption that people will do what they say they will do. Their methods are effective in counting heads or packages, but not in predetermining consumer reactions.

Those who have been educated in clinical psychology keep on using the methods of clinical psychology to determine how normal men and women react to a specific product or selling tool. These methods cannot produce correct answers to marketing problems.

Marketing researchers who have orientation in sociology concentrate on consumer social classes. The consumer classification is necessary, but not sufficient, for getting marketing answers.

Each type of researcher has his personal yardstick and tries to fit the problem to his subjective measuring device. A personal yardstick is not a reliable measuring tool.

To a problem-directed marketing researcher, research methodology is simple. The problem-directed researcher defines the problem and uses the method or technique that will provide the correct answer in the shortest time at the lowest cost. But many marketing researchers are not problem-directed.

A problem-directed researcher knows that marketing research must provide for management both qualitative and quantitative information. Either one alone cannot serve as a basis for marketing decision. But many market researchers concentrate on qualitative factors and others stress only numbers of consumers.

All consumers do not have the same preferences, and behavior of consumers is determined by factors other than economic. Sociological classification of consumers is as important as economic. A teacher earning $150 a week does not buy all of the same things that a bricklayer earning the same amount buys; the teacher may attend a concert, theater or lecture; the bricklayer may go to a tavern. The teacher is more likely to prefer a soft drink or wine; the bricklayer's preference may be beer. Income, therefore, should not be the only basis for classification of consumers. Consumer classification should be socio-economic, not merely sociological or economic.

Present-day marketing deals mostly with the psychological aspects of products. The practical or functional aspects are generally not much different from competitive products.

To succeed in business, you have to make sure, first of all, that the product is of high quality, in accordance with the consumers' concept of quality or at least equal in quality to competitors' products. The consumers' concept of quality is often psychological.

Then you must be concerned with the package. You must predetermine the effect of the psychologically significant components of the package—brand name, logo, symbol, color and design with the functional aspects of the package, with the material (glass, plastic, steel, aluminum, paper) and whether it should be transparent or opaque. Also, you must predetermine the total effectiveness of the package.

Now, you must take up the advertising with the advertising agency. You must make sure that the theme can stand on its own, without the aid of graphics and sound. Also, you should determine the effectiveness of the sound and the graphics. Then you must predetermine the total effect of the ad or commercial.

Media—television, radio, newspapers, magazines and billboards—should be considered. We can appeal to consumers through the ear (radio) or the eye (print) or both to the ear and eye at the same time (television).

The most important aspect of advertising is motivating communication. Originality, uniqueness, and creativity are the means; motivating communication is the essence of effective advertising. But we cannot have effective communication without creativity.

We invite failure if we do not understand that the most important element in advertising is motivating communication and that creativity or originality is the only means for producing effective communication.

The theme or appeal is the most vital factor in advertising, because a poor theme, which means a poor concept, cannot be imbued with motivating power. Although it is true that the best theme can be ruined by poor graphics or inferior presentation, we must keep in mind that the theme or basic concept is the foundation for an effective ad.

We can predetermine the effectiveness of a theme or an appeal through research that is conducted on an unconscious level. We present a number of themes to representative consumers. The consumers are asked to respond to products or brands, not to themes.

The test is designed to reveal how consumers react to four or five competitive products as they are represented by the four or five themes. Each theme represents a product or brand; the theme characterizes the "brand" or "product."

Unfortunately, most ad agencies do not want to test themes. There is considerable so-called research that has resulted in marketing failures, because the agencies tested the ads or commercials to determine which of a number has the greatest appeal or which of several is recalled by most people. The failure was due to bad research, bad because it makes critics out of consumers, permitting the representative consumer to step out of his role as a consumer and assume the role of a critic; bad because it is conducted on the assumption that effective advertising has to be recalled consciously.

If research is conducted on the assumption that consumers are interested in ads or packages, it leads to failure. If a researcher assumes that consumers are judges of ads or packages, he is inviting failure. If the practitioner of marketing research believes an ad that has great memorability is also an effective ad, he is courting failure. If one who conducts research believes a package that rates high aesthetically is necessarily an effective package, he is promoting failure.

Most failures in marketing research are caused by researchers who assume that consumers can or will give correct answers to direct questions.

The following shows that people's behavior is not predictable by their answers to direct questions; people either don't know what they will do or they think they know but don't think they should tell you.

In a test of three detergent packages, after using the detergents from all three packages, 60 percent of the users reported that one of the packages contained a heavy-duty detergent; 27 percent thought that one of the other packages was for heavy duty; 13 percent found the three detergents about the same. Actually, all three detergents were the same; only the packages were different.

In direct interviews, people say that they are not interested in ads, but the following shows that ads are of interest.

During World War II, a magazine was offered to a group of soldiers in two editions—the regular issue and a special overseas edition from which the ads were eliminated. Out of about 300 men, only 22 wanted the much smaller and lighter weight overseas edition without the ads; over 280 men wanted the regular edition, although they were made aware that they were being shipped overseas and that the heavier magazines would be an added burden.

A number of studies showed that individuals who claimed that they were not influenced by advertising bought only widely advertised products. Their conscious minds rejected advertising, but their behavior showed that they were influenced by it, subliminally or unconsciously.

The following is a report of one of the many studies showing that people cannot tell you what they have seen.

Men and women were given eye-movement tests on three pages of a newspaper; after twenty-four hours the subjects were interviewed on what they had seen and read the previous day.

The following shows the verbalized responses and what they had actually seen as recorded by the eye-movement camera.

For areas seen (as revealed by the eye-movement camera), claims of having seen the areas were 68 percent for page 1, 62 percent for page 2, and 68 percent for page 3.

For areas partially seen (as revealed by the eye-movement camera), claims of having seen the areas were 60 percent for page 1, 47 percent for page 2, and 61 percent for page 3.

For areas not seen (as revealed by the eye-movement camera), claims of having seen the areas were 29 percent for page 1, 11 percent for page 2, and 26 percent for page 3.

This study shows that when people are asked to recall what they have seen, there is a considerable difference between what they say they saw and what they actually saw, as recorded by an instrument.

In another study with a large sample of consumers, the respondents were asked to indicate where they had seen each of twelve products advertised—television, newspaper, or magazine.

Twenty-two percent of the respondents said that they had seen Hershey chocolate on television, 39 percent said they had seen it advertised in the newspapers and 52 percent said they had seen it advertised in magazines. This product had not been advertised in any of these media.

Dole Pineapple, Clapp's Baby Food, Cannon Towels, Cadillac cars and Champion Spark Plugs have not had advertising time purchased for them on television (according to Standard Advertising Register). However, from 22 percent to

46 percent of the respondents reported that they had seen these products advertised on television.

This shows that many people are not able to tell where they saw a product advertised. It also means that individuals often are not aware which advertising source motivated them to buy a product or how they were motivated.

We have much evidence that people remember little of what they see and generally are not aware whether they have or have not seen an ad.

A proof of an unpublished ad was shown to women and they were asked, "Have you seen this ad before?" Sixteen percent said they had. Yet they could not have seen it because it had never appeared in any publication.

A few weeks later the same persons were shown the same ad proof sheet and were asked the same question. Only 22 percent of those who had seen the ad before said they remembered it.

The proof sheet dealt with a cosmetic. The respondents were not trying to be misleading. No doubt they answered the question honestly, but their answers showed that most of them could not recall the ad.

We have just as much evidence that people cannot predict what they will do in the future. It was reported that Elmo Roper conducted a survey to forecast public response to *Life* magazine. The study showed that *Life* magazine would not be a success. We all know that there was something wrong with the prediction.

The national elections of 1948 were an outstanding example of the unreliability of polling methods. Dr. Gallup, Mr. Roper, and other pollsters failed to predict the election results because many just didn't know or would not say how they would vote. People could tell the interviewer what they thought they would do when they walked into the voting booth, and sometimes they did. What people think they will do and what they actually do when they have to act are often entirely different.

Also, a factor that makes polling unreliable is unwillingness to give true information. To a pollster's question, "Have you borrowed money from a personal loan company?" a poll showed that no one had. But the loan company's records showed that all those interviewed had borrowed money.

Another, now well-known, example is a survey on what magazines people read. To the question, "What magazines do you read?" a poll indicated that the *Atlantic* had six times its actual circulation and that a pulp magazine, printed in the millions, had poor circulation. Obviously, many of those questioned were unwilling to go on record as lowbrow although they enjoyed reading "lowbrow" publications.

There is conclusive evidence that research of the polling type, based on direct questions, is not a reliable tool because (1) people do not have the ability to give the right information, and (2) people are not always willing to give the right information.

Research that is conducted on an unconscious level with controls is the only kind of research that is reliable.

Judgment enters into the research picture when a decision has to be made on what should or should not be tested. Judgment based on experience has to be used in designing the test for the particular problem. It is again needed in interpreting the research results and in making effective use of the findings.

Studies show that consumers' motivations remain relatively the same for long periods of time. People's interests change very little under normal socio-economic conditions. A great social or economic change has a great effect on people's behavior, and changes their wants.

The behavior of consumers cannot be predicted, if a great social or economic change has taken place between the time of the study of consumer attitudes and the time of marketing. But, under normal socio-economic conditions, consumers' behavior in relation to a product or a specific aspect of a product can definitely be predicted.

However, competition can get into the marketing arena, thus cutting the market share and making necessary a revision in the product, price, package, or advertising.

In the June 24, 1960, issue of *Printers' Ink,* George Gallup, the well-known pollster, expressed his views on marketing research. If I had not seen the date of the publication, I would have thought the article was written in 1900, instead of 1960. The name Gallup belongs to the contemporary scene, but the statements made by Gallup were pre-Freudian and pre-Planckian. They seemed strange in our age of the "subconscious mind and nondeterministic physics."

There is, of course, nothing wrong in the Gallup method of handling statistics. His audits no doubt are accurate. Here again the trouble is caused by the pollsters assuming that people can or will give true answers to direct questions.

George Gallup knows, according to the article in *Printers' Ink,* "Why questions have a built-in Chinese Wall," that people can't tell you "why," but at the same time he says that "only 5 percent of the buying decisions are made on the unconscious level" and that "95 percent of the buying decisions are consciously reached."

This means he believes 95 percent of the housewives are aware that the only difference between some brands is the package, the trademark, the design, or the color. It means he thinks that the average shopper is aware she is being motivated by the package or advertising sales appeal.

Then Dr. Gallup discussed the merits of "getting consumers to reconstruct the buying decision, of getting them to reconstruct step by step the events leading up to a particular purchase."

He said further: "Consumers are good reporters and they are accurate reporters."

Of course, if the average shopper were conscious of the reasons for making a purchase, she could reconstruct it. But she does not know the reasons for making her choices in the marketplace.

The evidence is that people are not good or accurate reporters.

Subscribers to *True Story Magazine* were asked to check a list of magazines they received in their homes. About 10 percent checked that they were getting *True Story Magazine*. Almost 90 percent checked the publications that had status. Yet Dr. Gallup says you can rely on people giving the right information.

Consumers were asked where they had seen Hershey chocolate advertised. About 50 percent said they had seen it advertised in magazines and about 25 percent said television. Hershey was not advertised in either medium. Yet Dr. Gallup claims that consumers can give accurate reports.

Shoppers stated in an interview in a supermarket that they had seen certain packages of dry milk in the supermarket a day to a week before the packages were put on the store shelves. They actually could have seen those packages only in the newspapers, the day before the interview in the store. Yet Dr. Gallup states that people are accurate reporters.

Then there is, of course, sensation transference; consumers transferring to the product the qualities or attributes of its package. Yet Dr. Gallup finds that asking consumers questions results in correct answers.

Shoppers report that they have seen products advertised on television that never have been advertised there. They claim to have seen products advertised in magazines that never have been so advertised. Some buy only advertised products, but are not aware that they have seen the printed ads or the filmed commercials.

Yet Dr. Gallup believes that consumers are good and accurate reporters.

Many admen, David Ogilvy among them, say that Dr. Gallup conducts marketing research—research to determine the effectiveness of marketing tools for selling products that differ from competitive products only in psychologically meaningful aspects.

Over a quarter of a century ago, in 1936, to be exact, I conducted studies in "Communication." In one study, people were asked why they live in houses and why they wear clothes.

Almost all the men and women gave the same answers. They said they lived in houses to keep out the cold, to keep out the rain and to maintain privacy.

They all said, without exception, that they wore clothes to keep warm (in winter), to keep from getting sunburned (in summer), and most of all to cover their nakedness. "To be decent," some actually said.

The respondents thus gave us their concepts and the specifications for a house and for wearing apparel.

We met their specifications. We offered house-size boxes in which families of four and six individuals could sleep. These large boxes met all the specifications for a home given to us by the respondents. The boxes were guaranteed waterproof. They were guaranteed to provide warmth in temperatures twenty degrees below zero, and they provided absolute privacy. There were small windows at the top of the walls. On the inside there were removable partitions. Each "home" was offered for $1,000, not $20,000, the price of a cottage.

There were no buyers. Obviously, there are other reasons for living in a home than those given to us by the respondents. But the respondents could not give us those reasons.

We offered an Eskimo outfit of fur, guaranteed to keep anyone warm in twenty-below-zero temperatures, and also a long cotton shirt that was guaranteed to cover "nakedness" and to keep the sun away from the skin.

But we had no buyers, although both the Eskimo outfit and the cotton coverall were offered at bargain prices. These garments met all the specifications given to us by the respondents, but still they were not acceptable to them.

Obviously, people wear clothes for reasons other than to keep warm, keep the sun away, or because of modesty. But the respondents could not give us those reasons.

There are psychosocial reasons for living in houses and for

wearing clothes. There are psychosocial reasons for living in certain kinds of houses or apartments and for wearing certain styles of clothes. The respondents could not give us those reasons.

I learned this over a quarter of a century ago. Does Dr. Gallup think that now people are different, that now people actually can tell why they buy one brand of coffee instead of another, why they buy one kind of soap instead of another, why they buy one garment instead of another, or why they buy a certain house? Does he really believe that an interviewer can evaluate the reasons?

There has been as much progress made in the behavioral sciences as in the field of physics. But most marketing researchers have not observed the progress that has been made in recent years in the behavioral sciences or they cannot break away from their useless, frozen frame of reference.

A psychologically oriented researcher knows that women, and also men, "are good" at rationalizing their decisions, not at stating the true motives for their actions.

Psychologically oriented researchers have found that the actual facts about buying decisions are exactly the opposite from Dr. Gallup's ideas of behavior in a shopping situation. Ninety-five percent of buying decisions are made on an unconscious level, 5 percent are made on a conscious level.

This means that about 95 percent of shoppers are not conscious of the fact that they are motivated by the package, the brand symbol, or the color. About 5 percent are aware only of product quality, and consciously disregard the psychological factors, such as design, color, and other elements that have no actual relationship to the quality of the product.

I must add that this ratio of conscious and unconscious behavior is prevalent not only in the supermarket. Even in love and in making a choice for marriage, about 95 percent of decisions are made emotionally, on an unconscious level, and only about 5 percent on a conscious and rational basis.

People are not aware of the psychological motivating factors. They certainly cannot verbalize about them. They can tell no more about the psychosocial factors for buying cars than they can for buying homes and wearing apparel.

Actually, they can tell less about cars. Many individuals recognize the traditional or historical aspects of dwellings and attire. Automobiles have no tradition.

Many a young man marries a girl because he becomes infatuated with her cute nose, her blonde hair, or a specific part of her anatomy. But what is the reason he gives for marrying the girl? Her remarkable character. Why should we expect him to give us any more accurate information about his reason for buying a car?

Because most buying decisions are made on an unconscious level, marketing research, intended to determine attitudes of consumers toward a product and to measure potential acceptance of the product by consumers, has to be conducted on an unconscious level. This means that the responses to questions about the package, symbol, ad, or the product itself are not influenced by ego involvement and status-seeking; the responses reveal attitudes toward the product, not the package it is in, or its advertising.

Tests that are conducted on an unconscious level are the only valid tests for determining consumers' attitudes toward the product or marketing tool and for predicting the potential market for the product.

Specifically, marketing research should determine the effectiveness of the symbol, package, logo, design, or marketing theme, as a selling tool, not as a work of art. The test has to be designed to reveal the character, degree, and nature of the communication, not its aesthetic quality or degree of originality. Creativity should be considered always a means, not an end.

People cannot give accurate answers to direct questions about symbols, packages, brand names, themes, etc., because they are not aware that the graphic or verbal elements have an effect on them.

Also, consumers will not give accurate answers to direct questions because they normally give answers that will put them in a favorable light.

Direct questions are not a reliable means of obtaining accurate information, because people give rational or prestigious answers to direct questions or because, unconsciously, they transfer the sensations from the package to the contents or from the ad to the product; they are not aware that the package or ad influences them.

No housewife will say, in response to a direct question, that she buys a specific brand of food because she likes the package. To a direct question, she says that she likes the product. Yet she passes up a competitive product of comparable quality.

Marketing research, therefore, must be conducted on an unconscious level. The research has to be designed to disclose the consumer's unconscious feelings and true attitudes.

Yet, most marketing research consists of polling and direct interviewing. Most of the research concentrates on numbers and disregards the psychological factors in marketing psychological satisfactions.

10

TEST MARKETS
ARE NOT RELIABLE

LARGELY BECAUSE marketers do not fully understand the psychological factors, many rely on test markets. Recently, some have found test markets unreliable.

"FIGURES DON'T LIE? Test-Market Results Are Clouded by 'Spoiler' Tactics of Competitors—Critics Say 'Predictive' Value is Lost" is the title of an article by Ted Stanton that appeared in the *Wall Street Journal* on May 24, 1966.

Stanton said: "The heightened competition in test markets has become disquieting to many marketing men. They fear it is distorting the sales results obtained in these experiments, thereby reducing the effectiveness of an important research tool widely used by makers of consumer products; far too many products that presumably have done well in test markets are proving to be busts in general distribution, they note, and failures in the test-market phase itself are too frequent. So marketing men are warning manufacturers to read their test-market results with a more critical eye—and to use other methods as well to try to predict a product's reception by the fickle mass public."

He pointed out that supermarket executives are demanding more data to help them choose products that are pressed on them by manufacturers. He quotes Theodore A. Von Der Ahe, president of Von's Grocery Company, a Southern California supermarket chain, who estimates that a Von's store carries about 8,500 grocery items and 6,500 more in other departments. About 4,000 to 5,000 new items are offered to the store every year; of these only about 1,000 can be accepted.

A supermarket executive in Arizona says "a competitive response, and more often deliberate clear-cut distortion" by competitors, is a far from unique accompaniment to the launching of a new product in test markets.

Stanton said the marketing manager of a large household products company told him that competitors will do anything possible to muddy test-market sales figures. "They make special price deals on their own products with the stores, they expand their advertising heavily, and they'll even do things like yanking the number-one brand off the shelves temporarily just to foul up sales comparisons. One firm even bought up most of the available radio and TV spots when word leaked out we were going into a city for test marketing." This marketing manager told Stanton: "Of course, we do pretty much the same things ourselves when we can."

The writer quoted another food company executive: "A coffee company put its premium-grade coffee in a fancy canister, raised the price a few cents, and tried it out in one large city. A rival firm promptly copied the canister design, filled it with its cheapest-grade coffee, cut the price, and put it into the same city."

Stanton quoted Arthur Kaponen, director of marketing research for Colgate-Palmolive Company, a big test marketer: "A lot of money spent on these campaigns is wasted. In projecting test market results, 'the apparent reality is more often than not an illusion.' The competition may do 'everything it can to throw up a smoke screen and obscure results.' "

This "jamming" or "spoiling" of a rival's testing is common and is accepted by most big marketers. Much of it is intentional, but some of it results from sheer jostling among many new products introduced at roughly the same time into a restricted number of test cities.

The writer said further: "Certainly there have been bombs aplenty among products exposed to the mass public after seemingly successful test marketing. Recently, General Foods dropped from its Good Seasons line some ready-mix gravies and sauces that had gone through testing and into national distribution. A specialty soap, successfully tested, flopped in the national market after the manufacturer built a plant especially to produce it; the loss ran into millions of dollars.

"Sometimes testing procedures fail to take into account important product characteristics. One baking company put a new cookie into mass markets after it did well in test cities, but nationally, it was a sales disaster. 'The cookie was fine if you ate it fresh,' laments a company executive, 'but unfortunately, after it sat on the shelf awhile, it tasted just like soap.' In the test markets, the company was able to make more frequent deliveries and watch the supermarket shelves more closely than it could when national distribution began.

"A growing number of consumer products marketers now are doing some inexpensive, preliminary testing on a small number of consumers before deciding even to go into a test market. Since last fall, for example, National Biscuit Company has been submitting prototypes of some new products to an informal panel of consumers. If they judge the product has potential, it is tested in homes. Only after these steps is it submitted to a test market."

Then Stanton reported that according to one executive of a major corporation, the most significant advance in pre-market testing is "concept testing"—going directly to the consumer to get her reaction to the idea of the product sometimes before that product is even developed. "General Foods and an increasing number of other companies are using this approach."

Stanton concluded his article in the *Wall Street Journal:* "It's likely, however, that these methods will supplement test marketing, not replace it. Imperfect as it may be, test marketing does put the product before the critical eye of the shopper in a genuine buying environment—something the other methods cannot. Clay Rohrbach, marketing vice president of Borden Foods Company, divison of Borden Company, says: 'You simply don't know what will happen to a product unless you test-market.' Then he adds: 'Of course, you may not know for sure afterward, either.' "

For over twenty years I have been pointing out that test markets are not reliable means for predicting sales.

Stanton has been told of "concept testing" and "informal panels of small numbers of consumers." Twenty years ago I was shocked by the fact that marketers based their marketing programs on such fallacious concepts. I am no longer shocked. Now, I know that the difference between big men and little men is that the big ones make bigger mistakes.

The more experience a man has, the more likely he is to follow the track of his experience, even if now it may lead him to disaster. He knows what he knows and he does not want to know anything else. He does not want to be confused by facts, if the facts are new, not within his own experience, not in his frame of reference.

"Concept testing" is nonsense. One who has orientation in the behavioral sciences knows that only creative people and intellectuals deal in concepts. The masses of consumers respond to things, not to concepts.

The concept of air conditioning could not be sold to the masses. The concept of the airplane could not be sold to the masses. Men of vision have concepts that are the basis for things. The great masses of consumers can respond only to the things.

When consumers were asked about a dozen years ago whether they would buy yellow margarine, if it were made available, over 90 percent said they would not; they used only butter. (But when we served yellow margarine and white butter, they enjoyed the margarine and rejected the butter.) When consumers were asked whether they would use instant coffee, over 90 percent said they would not; they brewed their coffee. When consumers were asked whether they would buy a new magazine called *Life,* the great majority said no; they had all the magazines they wanted. When consumers were asked what kind of car they wanted and the manufacturer produced the kind of car the car owners said they wanted, the car failed because the people would not buy the kind of car they said they wanted.

You invite failure if you base a marketing program on testing concepts with consumers. You must test the real thing. You cannot talk about function and have it meaningful. You cannot describe styling or design and get the same reaction as to actual styling or design. You cannot name a color and get the same reaction as to the actual color.

If you want to succeed in business, don't rely on "concept-testing." Test the thing—the product or "image."

How about consumer panels? They, too, are poison. The marketing executive who relies on panels of consumers, in small or large numbers, is asking for trouble.

In consumer panels, the consumers are no longer samples of consumers—they are educated consumers. They are experts; they no longer behave as consumers. What these consumers tell you is not equal to what they themselves will do; their responses are not representative of consumers in the marketplace.

Stanton's article merely shows that many big marketing men make big mistakes, because they still think in terms of a society of scarcity. It reveals that they do not understand consumer behavior in an affluent society. It discloses that executives have not grasped the fact that in an affluent society people largely buy psychological satisfactions, not biological necessities, and, therefore, psychological devices must be used in marketing research and in planning marketing programs.

A market test, even if it is not mutilated by competition, is not truly a test, because in a true test, only one factor can be tested at a time.

Scientific procedure demands that the brand name be tested by itself, the logo by itself, the color by itself; then the package should be tested as a whole, because the whole is not the same as the sum of the parts—the composition of the components or the organization is a factor. The ad has a theme and graphics; each must be tested separately and then the whole ad has to be tested.

The cost of a test market is many times greater than any marketing research and the test market produces merely a black or white answer. If the brand fails in a test market, there is no way of knowing whether the product itself was unacceptable to consumers, whether the package did not communicate effectively, whether some element of the package— logo, symbol, color—was wrong, or whether the advertising had a negative effect.

Usually, executives are wrong about the reasons for marketing failures because they seek rational reasons for the failure, whereas actually the reason is usually a psychological one.

Marketing failure because of a socio-economic upheaval cannot be prevented. Also, introduction of a great product improvement by a competitor cannot be predicted by any pretesting. Most marketing failures, however, are caused by psychological factors in packaging and advertising. Marketing failure because of a bad package or because of bad advertising can be prevented. The degree of effectiveness of a brand name, symbol, logo, color, marketing theme or ad graphics can be pre-determined by tests conducted on an unconscious level, not in a test market.

11

SELLING PSYCHOLOGICAL SATISFACTIONS

PRESENT-DAY BUSINESSMEN usually fail because they cannot deal with the new conditions, with the conditions of an affluent society. A man who was brought up in a society of scarcity cannot easily begin to think in terms of an affluent society. If he began his business in selling biological necessities for daily life, he generally assumes that he can be successful in selling psychological wants by using the same marketing methods. He assumes that if they have been successful in selling bread and hamburger they can be equally successful in selling shrimps and steak.

But people do not buy bread and hamburger for the same reasons they buy shrimps and steak. Consumers do not buy herring for the same reasons they buy lobster.

In the past, there were few buyers of steak and lobster; now about 50 percent of our population can afford to buy, and most of them do buy, steak and/or lobster.

As recently as a quarter of a century ago, the majority of our people went to a restaurant because they were hungry; now they go to a restaurant for pleasure, to enjoy dining.

Dining out is not merely eating: it is sociability; it is enjoyable eating.

Homes are not mere shelters; they are designed and decorated. Clothes are not bought for keeping warm but for style and design.

At the beginning of the century, a man bought a car because he needed transportation; he now buys an attractively styled car that also gives him transportation; the transportation is taken for granted.

Selling pleasure—art, design, styling, aesthetics, psychological wants—is not the same as selling shelter or transportation. We must employ psychological means for selling psychologically meaningful goods—exotic foods, luxurious home furnishings, stylish clothes, cars that serve as status symbols.

Functionally, competitive products are generally alike. From a practical or performance aspect, competitive products differ very little.

You can have a marketing advantage only in the aspect that is psychologically significant. This means that, from a rational point of view, it may be insignificant. Because it is insignificant from a practical aspect, it probably is not in the marketer's frame of reference and he is likely to overlook it.

The most popular car differs from an unpopular car in functionally insignificant aspects—styling, name. You can provide the examples. The best selling cake-mix differs from the poorest selling cake-mix in insignificant culinary attributes.

The functionally or rationally insignificant is often psychologically very significant; therefore it is highly significant in marketing.

The greatest profits result from the insignificant. This reality was most difficult for me to accept and it may be difficult for you to recognize.

Most products are produced to satisfy psychological wants, not biological needs. In the modern supermarket, over 90 percent of the products are for satisfying psychological wants.

In order to maintain health, we must eat a variety of foods: meat or fish, vegetables such as cabbage or onion, bread, salt, and some oil and vinegar. These commodities do not comprise even 10 percent of the products in an up-to-date supermarket. We now have all sorts of cake-mixes, numerous desserts, a great variety of packaged products. All these are produced to satisfy psychological wants.

These products are designed for pleasure, not for maintaining life. They are the products of a society of abundance. They are the ingredients of an affluent society. They have psychological values.

They can be sold by employing psychological devices. Psychological aspects are in all phases of our life, and psychological factors are involved in marketing all consumer products.

A man can keep his trousers up with a string or rope, or he can buy a belt for $1, $5, $10, or $15. The difference between a $15 and $1 belt is not in the ability of the belt to keep your pants up. The difference is psychological. The most costly belt is unique, different; it is endowed with status because it is rare and because it has unique characteristics. These unique qualities have psychological appeal. Although they have no functional attributes, they have psychologically significant values.

In underdeveloped societies most people have to struggle to earn a living; most are concerned about survival. In an affluent society like ours, most people are concerned with products that have psychological appeal. About 90 percent of our incomes are spent on psychological satisfactions—styling, design, color.

To cover our bodies, we need only coveralls and a sheepskin or other warm garment for winter. But we spend our money on dress clothes, sports clothes, and business clothes. We could live in shacks. But we want homes with interior decoration. Cars with luxurious interiors are also in great demand.

Although we live in a society of abundance, we nevertheless still think in terms of a society of scarcity, because we have been conditioned or educated in traditional behavior patterns. We have been taught to be economical, to be rational or practical.

We are attracted by psychological elements—design, color

—but we try to be, or try to give the impression that we are, practical.

The choices we make are irrationally motivated, but we seek rational reasons for making them. Generally, we are not aware that we are irrationally motivated. We think we are buying functional quality, whereas actually we are attracted by the styling. Sometimes, we are aware of our irrational behavior, but we cover up; we try to make ourselves appear rational.

This is why, in order to learn how people really feel about an object or a design, we must rely on motivation research; we must use testing methods borrowed from the behavioral sciences. Special techniques, not direct interviews, have to be used for learning of motivations about which individuals cannot or will not talk.

Only motivation research can get the correct answers to problems of selling psychological satisfactions.

Motivation researchers are interested in what people do and why they do it, not in what they say. There are a number of testing techniques used in motivation research: depth interviews, projective tests, sentence completion and association tests. All of these are borrowed from clinical psychology.

Some motivation research techniques are structured and some are unstructured. In a structured test, the questions are carefully designed and are exactly the same for all respondents. In an unstructured depth interview, the interviewer, who is generally a trained psychologist, makes up the specific questions as he interviews from a general outline; this kind of research depends greatly on the skill of the interviewer.

Because depth interviews are very costly, interviews with only a few individuals serve as a basis for drawing conclusions; the report does not contain significant statistics. The structured type of research depends on the design of the test, on the controls used in the design and in the administering of the test; also, consumer samples must consist of several hundred interviews.

In a structured, controlled association test, the respondents are asked to select alternatives among successive polar terms, such as bad, good; high quality, low quality. The results are in statistical form.

Structured association tests are used by some for measuring judgment. A scale of several positions is used between each pair of terms for the respondent to indicate intensity or depth. The scale between bad and good, for example, may show whether in the individual's judgment the object is bad, a little bad, almost good, or good. This is a four-point scale. Six, seven, eight, nine, or still larger scales are used by some academic researchers. This type of association test is an interesting intellectual exercise, but it is of no value in solving marketing problems.

The assumption that the average consumer uses a nine-point, seven-point, or four-point scale when she is in the supermarket reveals a lack of awareness of marketing realities. She believes she is reacting to the product. Actually, she is affected by the package; therefore, she cannot use a scale for judging the product, even if she is the kind of person who would.

We use controlled association tests. But our tests are conducted on an unconscious level. They do not reveal intensity of judgment of individual consumers, but their unconscious reactions. The respondents are called upon to react quickly and spontaneously, not to judge critically.

Unguarded reactions are necessary so that consumers' responses are equal to behavior in actual marketing situations. Consumers rarely judge critically in the supermarket; they react in black-and-white terms. They react to the package but they believe they react to the product; they take the package or leave it on the shelf.

A controlled association test is designed to reveal whether consumers react favorably or unfavorably and the reasons for their reactions.

The following questions about a marketing tool (name, symbol, package, theme, ad) are answered by a controlled association test:

1. How well liked is the product it represents (percentage of favorable associations)

2. What is liked and what is not liked about the product (number of specific favorable and unfavorable associations)

3. How much impact does it have (total number of responses)

4. How many want the product it represents (preference)

In a controlled association test, conducted on an unconscious level, the respondents react to polar terms (favorable and unfavorable words). There are two parts to this test: the actual test for the study and a control test chosen because it is of interest to the particular sample of consumers. In a test with housewives, the control test deals with a home interior or wearing apparel.

The response in a controlled association test is direct and spontaneous, equal to the behavior in a normal marketing situation, and reflects the true feelings of the individual. It reveals the actual attitudes.

Tests that are conducted on an unconscious level should not be confused with depth interviews in which the interviewer's particular skill plays a major role. The controlled association test is structured and is conducted in the same way by all interviewers.

The "control test" is a vital part of the controlled association test. It serves the following purposes:

1. It is designed to be of interest to the particular sample of consumers in order to get the respondent's cooperation.

2. It gives the test a noncommercial character and makes it possible for the respondent to give or check answers without inhibition, without defense mechanisms getting into the test situation.

3. It is a control on sampling. We have the correct answers

to the control test. If the answers to this test are wrong, we know that the consumers that were interviewed are not representative of the market.

Almost all products are sold in packages. The graphic image or form, abstract or realistic, is a psychological factor. The graphic image or form that plays a role in identifying the package serves as a symbol and is a vital element of the package. It is necessary to determine the degree of appeal and the connotations of each component.

Also, the psychological effect of the package as a whole is determined. This has to be established because the whole is different from, more or less than, the sum of its parts.

The psychological effect of a brand-identifying image, a color, or the package as a whole, is determined by means of a controlled association test. This test reveals the percentage of favorable responses and degree of consumer acceptance. The test discloses consumer attitudes toward the product in the package by means of specific favorable and/or unfavorable associations as well as declared preference.

In testing the effectiveness of a package, the respondents are asked to respond to the product, that is, to the contents, not to the package, because consumers are not aware that they are influenced by a package and they do not consider the package important. Unconsciously, they transfer the effect of the package to the product in it. Thus, an effective package communicates to the shopper that the product in the package is of high quality, whereas a bad package tells the shopper that the product it contains is of poor quality.

A major role of package research is to determine how much newness is needed to stimulate the interest of new consumers and how much of the old must be retained to maintain the confidence of old consumers.

The effectiveness of advertising is determined by following the same procedure used for measuring package effectiveness.

Twenty years of testing marketing tools on an unconscious level have shown that consumers are motivated by ads or commercials to buy a specific brand, but they do not remember the ad or commercial. Some remember the ad or commercial but are not motivated to buy the product it advertises. Our studies show conclusively that most people are generally not aware of being motivated by any specific ad or commercial.

We test several marketing themes (printed ads or filmed commercials) to determine the degree of communicating and motivating power each has, not which is remembered by the greatest number of people, because the effect of advertising is subliminal.

Many have asked how motivation research differs from clinical psychology. This question, I presume, is inspired by the fact that many clinical psychologists have entered the field of marketing research (just as many artists have entered the packaging and advertising fields).

A clinical psychologist has to predict how an individual will behave. I cannot predict how any one person will behave, but I can predict how 1,000 people will behave in relation to a specific stimulus (product, symbol, package, or statement). By choosing the 1,000 people so that they constitute a sample of 1,000,000 people, I can predict or predetermine the attitudes of 1,000,000 or more people toward the specific stimulus.

I can predict how many will react favorably and how many will react unfavorably to the object, symbol, or statement.

The research shows how many like it and how many dislike it, why they like it and why they dislike it. The research also reveals how many are indifferent to it, how many want it and how many do not want it.

A problem-directed marketing researcher knows that learning consumers' attitudes is not the same as taking inventory in a supermarket; he knows that in dealing with consumers the basic factor is psychological.

The researcher who is problem-directed does not use sentence completion tests because such tests reveal more about the respondent than about the stimulus—product, symbol, package, or ad. He does not use inkblots or other projective methods that put the respondent on the defensive and cause him to behave as he would not behave in a shopping situation. He does not ask the respondents to evaluate the product or selling tool on a judgment scale, because he knows that shoppers do not use judgment scales; they act in black-and-white terms; they react favorably or unfavorably.

A problem-directed researcher tests each component—symbol, logo, color—separately, because he knows that in order to learn the effect of each element, he must treat it as the only variable. Then he also tests the whole unit, because he knows that the whole is not equal to the sum of its parts. It can be more or less than the sum of the components; the composition or organization of the components is a vital factor.

The problem-directed marketing executive, like the problem-directed motivation researcher, knows that marketing research is simple and not costly; he knows he need not gamble, that the effectiveness of a brand name, symbol, logo, package, marketing theme, or ad can be predetermined.

For the big companies, we do not do product testing. We do conduct blind product tests for small companies if the product testing is part of a complete marketing program—package, advertising, etc.

In addition to determining the effectiveness of trademarks, brand names, packages, and advertising we have conducted "image" studies of corporations, department stores, specialty stores, hotels, restaurants, and communities.

In essence, motivation research seeks to learn what motivates individuals in making choices. Motivation researchers employ techniques designed to reach the unconscious or subconscious mind because preference generally is determined by factors of which the individual is not aware.

Individuals make decisions sometimes consciously, but more often unconsciously. Generally, people are not aware of what motivates them to buy one product or brand instead of another.

A person cannot tell that he is motivated by a form, color, pattern, or an arrangement, because he does not know that he is motivated by it.

Also, one generally tries to explain his actions in rational terms and normally he wants his behavior associated with socially acceptable standards. To direct questions the respondents try to give rational or prestigious answers, but they are irrational in their choices.

Direct interviewing or polling is not reliable for determining deep feelings and emotional reactions because people cannot or will not tell how they feel.

By using indirect methods of motivation research, we learn the true feelings of consumers and thus provide reliable information for businessmen.

The road to successful marketing is in awareness that the effectiveness of an ad or the effectiveness of a package is on an unconscious level.

To achieve marketing success, the marketer must be aware that the average consumer is not interested in either ads or packages; she (or he) is interested only in the product; she is not aware that she is influenced by the ad or by the package. She reacts to the product when she looks at the ad or package; she "sees" the product through the ad or through the package. She transfers the sensation from the ad or package to the product it represents; the product is her only interest. This is a reality the marketer must recognize, if he is to succeed.

You can succeed, if you think in a scientific manner, if you grasp just a few basic fundamentals about human behavior and some basic principles of research methodology.

The condition of our economy cannot be ascertained by any set of tests. But tests, conducted on an unconscious level, can ascertain whether your product will have consumer appeal, whether your package is effective, and whether your ads will cause consumers to want to buy your product.

The right kind of research never fails to provide marketing guidance. If the research is designed to reveal consumers' attitudes toward the product, as it is represented by the ad or the package, it can predetermine the effectiveness of the marketing tool—ad or package.

In effect, the total product consists of the combined ingredients or assembled units, produced for a practical purpose, plus the package and the advertising. Ingredients, package, and advertising are one to the consumer in our affluent society.

We can get consumers to "tell" us about the product when they are shown only the name, only the symbol, only the package, only the marketing theme, or only the ad, because to the consumers each of these represents the product and in effect is the product, the product that satisfies psychological needs or wants.

12

HOW TO
SUCCEED IN MARKETING

JAMES C. MILLER, Marketing Manager, International Register Company, wrote the following to a publication that had been featuring articles on the risks in marketing:

"As manufacturers of consumer products, we struggled for years with the problem of determining the reaction of the public to products. We believe we have finally reached a solution. For the past three years, we have been using a special type of indirect questioning which has proven to be accurate far beyond any other technique, inexpensive and quick.

"This type of research was not developed by us. It was developed by a nationally recognized research specialist who has twenty years of proven results in predictive testing. Our results have been a 50 percent increase in sales of a housewares item after a slight design change which was shown to have high consumer acceptance and the introduction of a new product which has become the number-one seller in its field after only eight months.

"We have no interest in publicity, but I would be happy to arrange an interview with the research specialist we use.

"I believe an article on this subject would be of enormous help to a great many readers."

The reply: A form letter expressing appreciation of his interest in the journal.

This journal of and for business is dedicated to the traditional concept that business is gambling and that the businessman always takes risks. It does not recognize the behavioral sciences as being in any way related to marketing. It is not interested in problem-solving by scientific means. Its emphasis is on tradition. It has no interest in marketing research because marketing research is not in the tradition of business.

To succeed in marketing, it is necessary to keep in mind some realities of marketing.

Most journals for businessmen put emphasis on advertising. More print is devoted to advertising than to any other phase of business because most money is spent on advertising.

In a society of scarcity, the purpose of advertising was merely to reach people. The objective was to announce and to familiarize. The more the name of a product was repeated, the more familiar it became.

But in an affluent society, familiarity is not enough. Now, consumers have to be motivated to want your product instead of a competitive one that practically or functionally is no different from yours.

Advertising is one of the four pillars of a marketing structure.

But most admen are not concerned with marketing structures.

Generally, admen have no marketing experience. But there are admen who have become successful marketing men and there are marketing men who have become successful admen.

Frequently, a great weakness found in ad agencies is the lack of marketing orientation. The lack of understanding of the total marketing structure causes admen to leave a void between the product and the advertising. The psychological elements of the package are disregarded; display is given no consideration.

Perhaps David Ogilvy is an example of a successful advertising man who does not understand the entire marketing structure. More likely he chooses to publicize only the advertising aspect for strategic reasons.

Most admen, however, actually have no concept of the entire marketing structure. They are completely immersed in advertising.

Packages are secondary considerations, if given any attention. Brand names are generally not their concern. The psychological powers of symbols are not known to them.

Marketing themes are agency concerns, not concerns of the client, according to most admen; the client should be shown only the completed ad or commercial, I was told by admen.

Marketing research? Many admen think it is an excellent aid in selling a program to clients. Some think it has value, if it confirms the creative man's opinion.

Kind of marketing research? Most ad agencies conduct playbacks or memorability tests and polls. A few employ depth interviewers. Most admen are against controlled motivation research either because they cannot control it or because they do not understand it; they believe it inhibits creativity. Few admen become successful marketing men.

However, W. A. Salo, a Canadian adman who made his mark in marketing before entering the advertising field, said this:

"While the Canadian market is not unlike that of the United States in geographical terms, the opportunity to bury major marketing investment mistakes in a market population of one-tenth the size is practically nonexistent, and this leads naturally to the caution of 'survival.'

"With the rapid trend away from a 'basic need' economy, consumer demand is becoming more heavily oriented to the need for luxury goods. Since such luxury goods satisfy the 'psychological' needs of man more than they do the 'functional' needs, a more sophisticated approach to these consumers is required. This sophistication, meaning an intimate knowledge of what is required in tested detail to reach discriminating consumers with optimal efficiency, has been the operating milieu of the marketing function in consumer goods companies for some time now, but the move from a staff service function to a line-operating management philosophy has not been possible in the past. This is mainly because a clear recognition of the need to turn managements' eyes away from internal operational cost reduction and more and more outward to environmental opportunities has not been so pressing as it now is in a market constantly seeking new profit-growth areas.

"The tight competitive nature of the package goods industry has speeded up the search for 'competitive edges' in all aspects of the business."

Marketers are divided into distinct classes:

1. Marketers who have not yet grasped the significance of marketing psychological satisfactions in our affluent society.

2. Marketers who know that there are aspects in present-day marketing that are not rational or are not purely practical, but who are not oriented in the behavioral sciences and cannot grasp the significance of symbolic power in images, colors, and designs.

3. Marketers who are aware of the power that can be implemented with graphic as well as with semantic means, but who do not know how to measure the effectiveness of the graphics and semantics produced by creative people.

4. Marketers who are highly sophisticated, but who are enslaved by "creativity," which they choose to, or are forced to, consider a "sacred cow"—an end in itself; they dare not submit creative contributions to research to determine communication effectiveness and motivating power.

5. Marketers who have suffered from bad research—the kind that was conducted on the premise that you can ask direct questions about psychological factors and get true answers, research that is designed without awareness of sensation transference and of respondents' defense mechanisms—ego involvements and status-seeking—research that is qualitatively or quantitatively deficient, research conducted without controls.

6. Marketers who believe that validated research is expensive, that they cannot afford it.

7. Marketers who are almost completely subjective and will never understand the significance of psychological factors.

8. Marketers who are problem-directed, who understand fully the marketing structure built on four pillars—product, package, price, advertising—and know that the character of every component can be predetermined through research, and that the research must be conducted on an unconscious level.

James C. Miller, Marketing Manager of International Register Company, is one of the outstanding marketing men. He knows well the marketing problems in an affluent society and he understands the principles of testing on an unconscious level. He said:

"There are three major factors affecting the consumer market in the U.S. today:

1. The population is growing. This population explosion has been given wide publicity.

2. The affluent segment of the population is increasing faster than the total population. Almost everyone has more discretionary income than ever before. Most marketing and sales people recognize this fact.

3. An increase in affluence changes an individual's taste.

It is to this latter factor that I think marketing men should direct their attention."

He said further: "The demand is for products with a 'quality' image. This is easy to say, but what is a 'quality' image and what is the product?

"The product is many things. It is the physical device itself, the package, the label, the advertisements, the catalog and the place in which it is sold. All of these are elements of the total product and must carry the 'quality' image.

"The 'quality' image is harder to define. It is not only reliability in use, it is the appearance of reliability; it is style; it is the appearance of function and usefulness. The product must be good, *and must look it.*

"The particular appearance which the market will interpret as an image of quality is not fixed. It is constantly changing. It is difficult to determine in advance, but it is not impossible.

"After repeated failures of direct questioning techniques in determining consumer reactions to products, many business executives have concluded that only by experience can one have any inkling of what the public will want. Since these same business executives have a good deal of experience themselves, it is not a difficult decision to make. I believe that experience is invaluable in handling salesmen, in making distribution decisions, and in many other ways. But it is of no help in determining how the American consumer will react toward a proposed product design.

"Nor can the designer predict this, much as he might wish to. Designing is essentially a subjective activity. Research is an objective function. The designer does not have taste which is typical of the American public. He is engaged in the conscious styling of products and has no way of telling what the subconscious reaction of the public will be to a new design. Only subconscious testing can do this.

" 'Experience' is still the major determinant of product appearance today. Since the market is constantly changing, past experience can have little value on tomorrow's design. Secondly, what many executives consider to be experience is merely a collection of prejudices acquired over a long period of time. Most people learn from experience, but unfortunately they often learn the wrong lesson."

He concluded: "It is said that the first step toward knowledge is the recognition of ignorance. The first step toward becoming a truly effective product innovator is the recognition that experience cannot tell how the consumer will react to the appearance of the product. The second step is the use of indirect questioning techniques by an experienced firm.

"As you know, we have taken these two steps. The results have proven the validity of this type of research. Our hope is that our competitors continue to use experience as their teacher."

Jim Miller shows in the above that he is truly an up-to-date marketing man. His great success is no accident.

F. R. Johnson, Merchandising Manager, T. Eaton Co., has a reputation in Canada as an outstanding marketer. His statement:

"Today we must be careful in dealing with the consumer market to understand that rational market techniques do not necessarily bring success with selling to consumers. If we were completely rational as a consumer nation we could satisfy the three basic economic needs of food, clothing and shelter on about 15 to 20 percent of our current gross national product. Therefore, it follows that approximately 80 to 85 percent of our total expenditures for goods and service is to satisfy other than basic or rational needs, in other words psychological needs."

To succeed in marketing you must avoid the spoilers of marketing programs. Executives who are dominated by subjectivity are spoilers. Ad writers who are interested in expressing themselves but not in communicating are spoilers. Package designers who consider their designs aesthetic expressions, not marketing tools, are spoilers. Researchers who conduct research by asking people direct questions about psychological factors are spoilers.

Above all, you must always guard against subjectivity.

The two major secrets of success are:

1. Test everything before putting it on the market—the product, brand name for new product, brand symbol, package design, color, marketing themes, ads.

2. Have all marketing research conducted on an unconscious level and with controls. The researcher should have the correct answer to the control with which to compare the test results. The control should be used by the researcher for validating the sample of consumers; if the answer to the control is

not right, he knows that the answer to the problem may not be right. The control is also an effective device for keeping the test on an unconscious level, so that the representative consumers express their real feelings and true attitudes.

By taking advantage of the two fundamental secrets of marketing success and by operating within the structure of the four pillars—product, package, advertising, price—on a solid foundation of brand exposure—distribution and display—you can be sure of having a substantial share of the market.

PART II

HOW I SUCCEED

1

DISCOVERY OF
SENSATION TRANSFERENCE

FROM 1935 to 1940, I directed a vast program in the field of perception. The projects conducted under the auspices of the Adult Education Program of the Chicago Board of Education gave me the opportunity to develop devices and methods for measuring reactions to design and color. Studies made with these devices showed that individuals were affected by images and colors in various ways, favorably and unfavorably, but they were not aware of the effect an image or a color had on them.

In 1945, I introduced the methods and techniques for determining how men and women react to designs and colors, graphic symbols, words and statements in relation to marketing and advertising.

My entry into the marketing research field was not planned. When I "finished my education," the Depression was upon us. Since I couldn't get a full-time job, I taught art, did some painting, and took graduate courses. I was ready to teach in the field of humanities, but there were no openings for teachers in this subject.

On the University of Chicago campus, where I lived in the same apartment for sixteen years, I was exposed to the Institute of Psycho-Analysis and to Alfred Korzybski, father of general semantics.

In 1934, I obtained a certificate to teach in the Chicago public schools, and I also renewed my contact with Elizabeth

Wells Robertson, director of art education for the Chicago public school system, who became a major influence in my life. (I met her when I was teaching at the Lewis Institute and she was a district art supervisor. I arranged scholarships for several "geniuses" she found in the public schools.) I asked her to read my paper which I had written as the preliminary draft for a dissertation. (I was urged by my supervisor to become a candidate for a Ph.D.) Three days later she called me and said she wanted to discuss the paper with me. The subject was "Objective Measurements of Ocular Sensations."

I pointed out in the dissertation that there were no objective measurements, that there were many concepts and assumptions, but there was no evidence of the effects specific images and colors produced. She told me that as chairman of the Art Education Section of the National Education Association (NEA) she wanted me to deliver this paper at the convention to be held in July, 1935, in Denver, Colorado.

Two weeks later I presented to her another paper of mine, titled "Social Forces In Art." At a later meeting, she told me that if I wished I could present the second paper at the convention, and she also informed me that she had given my paper, "Objective Measurements of Ocular Sensations," to Mr. William J. Bogan, Superintendent of Schools. (I presented it to the NEA convention in Milwaukee, Wisconsin, in the following year.)

My speech "Social Forces In Art" was a great success. I was the youngest speaker, 27 years of age. Other key speakers were Governor Paul V. McNutt, who had just returned from a term of service as governor of the Philippines, and Senator Jerald Nye, who was the author of a recently published book titled *Merchants of Death*. This was indeed a great opportunity for me.

I met Mr. Bogan at the convention. He told me he wanted to talk to me in Chicago.

Elizabeth Wells Robertson and William J. Bogan told me that a Smith-Hughes Fund was available to promote vocational education. If I was interested, I could conduct experiments in measurements of ocular sensations, and in developing a new phase in the graphic arts, as outlined in my dissertation.

I met with Robert White, Assistant Superintendent of Schools, who made all the arrangements to provide for the use of classrooms and other facilities. Part of this project consisted of conducting special classes in comparative arts for grammar school teachers who were seeking credits to enable them to conduct high school classes and for high school teachers to become qualified for positions in the junior colleges.

Before six months were over, Elizabeth Wells Robertson presented me with another program. She told me that the Board of Education had received a directive from Washington to set up an educational program for employing men and women who had no employment in private industry, but who were qualified in some way in the field of education. She asked me whether I would be interested in expanding my experimental program under Smith-Hughes by directing an art education project as a division of the Adult Educational Program of the Chicago Board of Education. Fifty percent of the money would be provided by the city school system and the other 50 percent by the Federal Government under FERA (Federal Emergency Relief Administration).

She introduced me to Vernon Bowyer who was the Director of the Adult Education Program. Bowyer immediately expressed interest in my project. Harry T. Fultz, the state supervisor of education for programs supported by the Federal Government, also showed interest.

The Adult Education Program opened up a still wider vista for me. It made the possibilities for experimentation far greater. Within a month I had a staff of almost 100 people. About half of them were to conduct classes for adults in community centers and school buildings. These classes for adults were a laboratory for the study of perception.

In one group were several German and Austrian refugees, a

psychologist who had worked intimately with Carl Jung, two men who were students of Sigmund Freud, and one who had worked with Rorschach. These men gave me much aid in designing tests and developing devices for measuring reactions to graphic creations or communications—works of art, symbols, abstract and realistic images, colors.

I established an in-service training program for the teaching staff and attempted to familiarize them with the psychological aspects of art expression. This was not easy because most of the art teachers were highly subjective. It was difficult to get them to think in scientific terms. It was almost impossible for the majority of the older members of the staff.

Also, I developed a system for art education, based on aesthetic, social, individual, and technical factors. For most of the teachers, it was difficult to follow this system, because art was considered by them purely a matter of self-expression.

The group that consisted mainly of German and Austrian refugees aided me in producing some tests, devices for measuring reactions and determining attitudes. These testing devices were designed to be used on an unconscious level, so that the respondents were not aware either of the purpose of the test or what the test was about.

Studies conducted with these devices during 1935–1940 disclosed that men and women are affected by abstract symbols —shapes and colors—but because people are not conscious of the effect that images and colors have on them, they cannot tell whether or how they are affected.

For example, in one study, a jar with a surface design of circles was thought to contain a product that was superior to the product in the container with a surface design of triangles. In this study, 200 women used two cold creams and were asked which they found to be superior. Almost 80 percent found that the cold cream in the container identified by "circle designs" was a much finer product. Yet, we knew that both jars actually contained the same product.

In my analysis of the results of this study, I pointed out that the people practiced sensation transference, that the women transferred the sensation from the design on the package to the product in the package.

We showed two panels with the geometric designs to over 1,000 women, and asked them which one they liked better, the triangle or the circle. The results were 50 percent for each. We concluded that the law of probability was operative, just as tossing a coin 1,000 times results in 50 percent heads.

In the direct-question part of the package study, the 1,000 women were asked which of the two package designs they preferred. The results were about 50-50; most of them stated that they did not consider the designs different in any essential way and that they were interested in the cold cream, not in the jar. This part of the study showed clearly that people were not conscious of being affected by design.

The same study contained a test in which the two containers differed only in color; one was pink and red and the other light and deep blue. Almost 80 percent of the respondents found the cold cream in the red and pink container of superior quality. This part of the study revealed that people are not conscious of being affected by color.

The study that followed produced similar results. Consumers found tea from one package was superior in quality to the tea in another package, yet the two teas differed only in that they were in different types of packages. In one part of the study the packages differed in shape, in the other part, the packages differed in surface design.

Such studies, conducted for almost five years (1935-1940), provided a wealth of information. These studies answered many of the questions that I raised in my dissertation. At that time, however, I did not think of any "practical" or commercial purpose.

The women and men attending adult education classes in various parts of the city were the consumers in the tests. Since those attending the classes were from all socio-economic levels (80 percent were women), they offered an excellent sample of the population of the Chicago area.

Low-income consumers attended classes in crafts, rug-weaving, and furniture making.

Consumers in high socio-economic classification attended classes in ceramics, sculpture, painting and design, and in art theory and art history. The refugees from countries dominated by Hitler also attended classes in English.

Directing perception studies, conducting in-service teacher training, and supervising classes kept me busy during the day; in the evening I conducted classes in comparative aesthetics with men and women who taught school during the day. These classes, under the Smith-Hughes Program, provided still another type of consumer sample. Studies revealed that teachers practiced sensation transference just as much as housewives.

I became deeply involved in the perception studies and in adult education, and I became interested in graphic art as communication.

Because I had a staff of able and reliable assistants, I could take time to do some writing. I expanded my dissertation, "Objective Measurements of Ocular Sensations," into a book. By 1938, I finished the manuscript and titled it *Living with Art.*

The fact that the manuscript had over 400 pages filled with data on perception made little impression on the publishers to whom I submitted it. Four publishers rejected the manuscript; one declared that it was too technical; the others said merely they did not think the book would have popular appeal. I then submitted the manuscript to Adolph Kroch, Chicago's outstanding bookman, book retailer and publisher. After reading the manuscript, he too told me it was too technical, that it contained too much scientific data, but he thought it had great merit and should be published in abbreviated form.

On Papa Kroch's recommendation, I eliminated the "scientific data" and reduced the manuscript to about 200 typed pages. His son, Carl, read the much edited manuscript and A. Kroch and Son decided to publish it themselves. *Living with Art* was published in 1940. It did not contain "scientific data" and was written in a simple and direct style, but it did not have a great sale, although it has been widely quoted.

Then came the attack on Pearl Harbor. As did many others, I offered my services to the war effort.

My Art Education Division of the Adult Education Program was asked to cooperate with the Federal Art Project in producing training aids for the Armed Forces. I terminated my Smith-Hughes Program.

Less than one year after the Japanese attack on Pearl Harbor, I received an invitation from the President of the United States; in other words, I was drafted.

After a month of time-wasting, I was assigned to teach photography and camouflage in a camp near Chicago, and three months later I was assigned to the Signal Corps, in the department of personnel training, with headquarters in the Civic Opera Building in Chicago.

At the Civic Opera Building, I met men who had been business executives before the war. They made me aware that my experience in measuring attitudes and my knowledge of devices for learning the unconscious motivation of people could be of great value to businessmen. Discussions with business-oriented men made me realize that the needs of the business world were no different from the needs of the Adult Education Program.

By using psychological means, I was able to promote an interest in adult education classes—painting, ceramics, literature, foreign languages, etc. I decided that the same psychological devices could be used for selling consumer goods.

When I was discharged from the Armed Forces in January of 1944, I made a definite decision not to return to the education field. Although my interest in adult education was great,

I now realized that in serving business I could greatly improve my standard of living.

Before the war, I gave some thought to the possibilities of predetermining the public acceptance of specific designs or works of art. I had no concept of the ways and means of marketing and had no vision of using research for measuring effectiveness of packages or advertising. But I thought of predetermining the salability of works of art—textiles, ceramics, paintings, drawings, etc.

I had conducted a number of studies to determine attitudes toward adult education in general and toward specific subjects, as well as toward works of art, including books and book jackets.

After the war, I had a picture of how I could serve business. But I knew almost nothing about how to run a business. I therefore set out to find a businessman who could run the organization while I occupied myself with directing marketing research.

2

BIRTH AND GROWTH OF THE
COLOR RESEARCH INSTITUTE

A FRIEND, WHO was in the insurance business, introduced
me to George D. Gaw, who was president of an envelope company and a well-known figure in Chicago. I explained to
George Gaw the basic principles of testing on an unconscious
level and showed him studies of geometric and realistic images and of colors. I could see that he was deeply impressed
and was particularly intrigued with the studies of colors.

"Businessmen and advertising men think they know much
about design and copy, but they recognize they know nothing
about color," he told me, and added that he was extremely
interested in color and had conducted some tests himself. He
also told me that he had a service organization called the Direct Mail Research Institute. He pulled out of a desk drawer a
number of bulletins that contained references to color; most
of them were reprints from popular magazines.

I enjoyed the evening at the Gaw home, but I did not know
whether Gaw was the man to introduce unconscious level research to the business world.

My second meeting with George D. Gaw was at his office.
The Direct Mail Research Institute office was at the National
Research Bureau. Gaw told me that NRB would sell any serv-
ice that had to do with research, and he proposed that we
form a company to provide guidance on color and design;
NRB would sell our services.

In September, 1944, the Color Research Institute set up business in an office next to the Direct Mail Research Institute, in the National Research Bureau Building, on the near North Side of Chicago. In January, 1945, we received our charter and were in full operation. George D. Gaw was president and director, Louis Cheskin was executive vice president and associate director, William Wood, President of the National Research Bureau, was director in charge of sales.

After two years it became apparent that the salesmen of the National Research Bureau could not sell our services. The concept of testing on an unconscious level was foreign to them. The words motivation research had no meaning to the salesmen.

We gave up the idea of the NRB selling our services and in the spring of 1947, we moved into the downtown area to be more centrally located, closer to business. We began to offer our research service on packaging and advertising by direct mail.

I had been concentrating on writing articles on marketing research and was preparing a book on color. I accepted the idea that the greatest need was for information on color. *Colors: What They Can Do for You* was published in 1947.

Indirect Approach to Market Reactions, the first report on our employment of motivation research techniques in solving marketing problems, was published in the *Harvard Business Review,* September, 1948. The article was reprinted and used as a mailing piece. It brought us many research assignments.

After publication of the article in the *Harvard Business Review* and of articles in a number of other business publications, our business grew. But the profit was low because we had too many generals and not enough soldiers on the payroll.

By 1948, we had more than a dozen clients on a retainer fee basis. They were small companies; most of them needed and wanted sales aids of various kinds. Gaw recruited them through his Direct Mail Research service. These companies used direct mail advertising. George Gaw was in contact with these companies both as director of CRI and director of DMRI. Mailings of reprints and reports of CRI research results brought in a steady flow of new clients, many small companies and a few large corporations.

We received an assignment from Standard Oil of Indiana to determine which of seven proposed signs for Standard gas stations would be most effective. One of the signs came out in our tests with scores of 86 in visibility, 81 in readability, and 94 in favorable associations. The sign that came out second highest rated 82 in visibility, 68 in readability, and 53 in favorable associations. We conducted the visibility and readability measurements at various distances, against a variety of backgrounds and under different weather conditions.

The Standard Oil sign that received high scores in our tests was adopted. This symbol (an oval in red, white, and blue with a torch in the center) is still the most effective in the oil industry.

Wesley I. Nunn, the advertising manager, and I worked together on many Standard Oil sales tools—packages and point of sale billboards. We also conducted an "image study" of the Standard Oil Company of Indiana.

Although getting business was the responsibility of George Gaw, I was not satisfied with the slow progress and I wanted to get more of the large corporations as clients. Early in 1947, I decided to write to a few of the big companies.

In my letter I suggested that they give special attention to their packages and told them that we had devices for predetermining which of a number of packages will draw the interest of the greatest number of shoppers in the store. I pointed out that our tests measured the effectiveness of the design and color; they revealed the degree of display effectiveness and the kind of psychological effect the package had. It took fourteen lines in four short paragraphs to present my case.

In reply to my letter, I received an invitation to make a presentation to Procter & Gamble.

George Gaw had to give a speech in Cincinnati on the power of color in direct mail. Both he and I knew that he could not explain our services. But nevertheless, I thought he should call on Procter & Gamble. He was not sure; perhaps; he would see after he got there; maybe after his talk. He did not feel that he could answer questions about the nature of the research. I knew that his comprehension of the methodology was very limited, so I did not press him.

It turned out that the deliberation was not necessary. When Charles Gerhart, packaging director of Procter & Gamble, learned that George D. Gaw, director of the Color Research Institute, was to speak before the Advertising Association, he decided to attend.

I prepared a typed speech for the press and an outline for Gaw. I never did know how much he followed the outline. But Charles Gerhart approached him after the speech and invited him to his office.

George Gaw returned with a can of Crisco and a request for me to outline the procedure, the cost, the time, and the type of information that we would provide. I immediately wrote a proposal and in four days received authorization to proceed.

Our tests were completed in two weeks. In my analysis and recommendation, I pointed out that the research clearly showed some glaring weaknesses in the package:

1. The package as a whole had poor visibility.
2. The brand name Crisco had poor readability.
3. The label caused excessive blinking and did not hold attention.

My recommendations in the report, April 4, 1947, were as follows:

The label should be redesigned with only the oval retained.

1. Simplify the lettering of the brand name Crisco.
2. Introduce red because it has a favorable association with cooking and with food and it will give greater visibility to the package.

3. Eliminate most, if not all, of the stars. In my opinion, the stars were responsible for the low eye-movement rating.

Charles Gerhart called me on the phone and told me he had found my report very illuminating and wanted me to come to Cincinnati to meet with his packaging committee. (I did not know, at the time, that such committees existed.)

The meeting with the packaging committee was a memorable one. There were fourteen men in the room. I learned that the packaging department was under the jurisdiction of the advertising department.

I proceeded to tell them about my experiments in 1935-1940, and I stressed that because of sensation transference, the package—not advertising—is the second most important factor in marketing, that the product, or rather its quality, was the first; advertising must sell the package; advertising cannot sell the product without the package because either the product has no form or its form lacks psychological appeal.

I said that the package incorporates both objective and subjective elements.

Display effectiveness is the objective aspect. Yellows and reds have greater visibility than blues and greens to all people regardless of their socio-economic status. Circles, ovals and triangles get immediate attention whereas nongeometric forms do not; the socio-economic status of the viewer is not a factor.

Images and colors also have psychological connotations through their symbolism. Reactions to symbols are subjective aspects that are largely governed by psychosocial or socio-economic factors. I did not use the word consumers on that occasion. I was in marketing but I still did not look upon people as consumers. I reported on some of the experimental studies (1935-1940) that revealed a great difference in the reactions and attitudes of various classes of people; attitudes were determined by ethnic origin, education, income, etc.

Then I proceeded to outline our ocular measurements of

involuntary reactions for determining the objective aspects of visibility, readability, and eye flow, which reveal the degree of display effectiveness a package has.

Also, I explained in brief the association tests that disclose the psychological connotations that the package, or any other visual unit, has. I pointed out that because of sensation transference, people cannot give true answers to a direct question about a package, and because people seek status, because of ego involvement and prestige identification, they frequently will not give the true answer, even if they think they know it. I gave examples of sensation transference and status seeking.

I was really wound up. I talked almost two hours. There was complete silence in the room. Then there were a few questions. I could see that most of the men were very interested in what I said, but one man was agitated. He thought I downgraded advertising. He said he did not agree that packaging comes before advertising or that it is even on a par with advertising in the marketing picture. I commented that packaging does not cost as much as advertising. But it is one of the pillars of a marketing structure; advertising without an effective package is largely wasted because the package has to be an integral part of the ad, and in the store, unless the package fulfills in its psychological connotations the promise of the advertising, the product is not taken home.

Advertising, I said, must sell the *image of the package* and the *concept of the product*. The package is the visual manifestation of the product. It is the symbol. It is the link that connects the product or brand with the shopper.

The man was not convinced. Gerhart did not come to my defense. I soon learned that in marketing circles this man's point of view was the prevailing one. (Even now, twenty years later, it still prevails.)

However, Charles Gerhart agreed with me, although he did not say so. He showed his point of view by giving me a number of packages to test. Procter & Gamble became a client of

CRI. All Procter & Gamble packages, many dozens of proposed designs, were put through our tests.

I enjoyed working with Charles Gerhart and his staff of bright designers. I found Charles Gerhart intelligent and stimulating. He impressed me with his social values and I had great respect for his point of view.

Another of my letters brought Quality Bakers of America (QBA). Robert Schaus, the advertising director, presented me with two problems: 1) to determine how effective as a trademark a portrait of a little girl, called Miss Sunbeam, would be. 2) Which of eight actors and actresses, if any, would be effective as an aid in selling bread.

Our study showed that "Miss Sunbeam" rated over 90 percent in favorable associations and that she would indeed be an effective marketing tool.

Another part of the study showed that some of the actresses could contribute a little to the marketing of bread, but that most of them would do more harm than good to the marketing program.

A few days after the report went out to QBA, I received a letter from Robert Schaus that took me off my feet. He told me that another motivation researcher was employed to get answers to the same two problems, that his answers to one of the problems agreed with mine but that his answers to the other problem were in disagreement with my conclusions.

The other researcher also found that most of the actors and actresses could not contribute to the marketing program. But he reported that Miss Sunbeam was not an effective trademark. He found that the little girl was "artificial and superficial," and because she was not considered "natural," he concluded that she was not a desirable symbol for Sunbeam. I was asked to explain the disagreement.

I pointed out in a lengthy letter that our studies are conducted on an unconscious level, that when we tested "Miss Sunbeam," with 800 mothers, we did not ask the mothers how they liked Miss Sunbeam as a trademark. We had evidence from experimental research, I said, that people are consciously interested only in products; they are not aware that they are affected by a trademark or package.

In one test, our interviewer showed the housewife two packages of bread; one had only the name Sunbeam on the wrapper, the other had the portrait of Miss Sunbeam, in addition to the Sunbeam logo. Our interviewer asked each respondent to mark a list of words and phrases, to indicate which loaf she thought "was superior in quality," "contained finer ingredients," "was better for her children," etc.

In another test, the respondent checked the terms on the response sheet after tasting a slice of bread from each package.

There was visual sensation transference in the first test, taste sensation transference in the second.

In both parts of the study, the Miss Sunbeam portrait upgraded the brand. This was obvious because it was the only difference between the two loaves of bread.

Miss Sunbeam has become the backbone of the Sunbeam marketing program and QBA is a marketing success story. It is a very successful marketing agency for over 100 bakeries.

In the eighteen years we have been conducting research for Quality Bakers of America, we have been involved in the development of dozens of packages and advertising campaigns.

I want to stress the fact that our research is conducted before the ad, billboard, or package appears on the market. QBA has other research conducted after the fact. Our purpose is to predetermine the effectiveness of a marketing tool, not to gather information on how effective it has been.

Two very interesting problems came from the Nestlé Company. One was on Nescafé, the other on Nestlé chocolate. Our research showed that a complete change of packaging of the coffee and the chocolate would have ruined both.

Our tests of the proposed designs for Nescafé showed that the new logo (lettering style of the name) downgraded the well-known brand, whereas a simplified version of the old logo increased the effectiveness of the package.

The proposed wrapper designs by European and American designers for Nestlé chocolate failed in all our tests. The research disclosed, however, that simplification of the lettering and changing the color, from a deep blue to a turquoise blue and from a cold deep red to a warm red, were great advantages. Our tests showed that these changes increased the favorable associations with the chocolate bar and the preference for Nestlé chocolates almost 100 percent.

These studies demonstrate the fallacy of the assumption, prevailing in marketing circles and upheld by most package designers, that a new package design is always an asset.

After about three years of conducting marketing research on an unconscious level, we established considerable validation in the marketplace. I reported our association with marketing successes in many articles and speeches. CRI ocular measurements and controlled, structured, association tests became well-known. But George Gaw was basically a salesman. He was trying to "sell" our services through direct mail. I thought our services should be "offered," not "sold." I insisted that businessmen buy our service when they become convinced of its value; we should merely present evidence of validation in the marketplace.

I insisted that we act like professionals and specialists. George Gaw maintained that I made people feel I was bestowing a great favor on them when I provided them with our service. I knew the value of our service; he really did not. I maintained that executives must feel at all times that they are masters of the situation, that they are doing the buying, not that they are being sold a bill of goods.

After five years of watching our marketing research "sold," I separated our service from salesmanship. In the fall of 1950, George Gaw retired and I reorganized CRI.

A bad experience in association with an engraving shop

caused me to conclude that CRI should not be concerned with the technical problems of printing. I therefore eliminated the technical service which had to do with color printing.

Also, I limited the Color Research Institute to providing clients with measurements of display effectiveness by conducting ocular measurements—visibility, readability, eye-movement tests—and providing color and image ratings on the basis of the accumulated information in our files.

To the public, the Color Research Institute has favorable connotations. CRI interviewers get full cooperation from consumers. For dealing with clients, however, CRI had the wrong "image." It did not represent our service; it did not put it in a true light.

Therefore, Louis Cheskin Associates (LCA) was created for serving clients. CRI conducts the field tests and LCA makes the analysis and recommendations.

3

BETTY CROCKER LEAPS
INTO FIRST POSITION

I HAD EVIDENCE that the greatest weakness in most marketing programs were the packages. I could see that millions of
dollars were being wasted on sterile ad campaigns, or on advertising that was generally impotent. But the packaging was
suffering from neglect, from lack of recognition by management that it was a vital factor in a marketing program.

Frequently, I went shopping with my wife on Saturdays to
study the packages in the supermarket. I noted that General
Mills had a number of cake-mixes. I also noted that it took
some time for me to learn how many different Betty Crocker
cake-mixes General Mills had. Each Betty Crocker package
had a different character. There was a complete lack of family
resemblance.

I had some statistical calculations and projections made and
these showed me that, all other factors being equal, the right
packages would at least double the sale of Betty Crocker cake-
mixes, and with the backing of an effective ad campaign the
right packages could bring as high as a 200 percent increase in
sales. I wrote this to Gordon Hughes, director of market research at General Mills. After an exchange of letters and after
I provided evidence of the sales results following package im-
provements in other companies, among them Procter & Gamble, I was retained to direct a repackaging program of Betty
Crocker products.

Our tests of the new packages showed that Betty Crocker

could expect a sales increase of 100 percent, all other factors remaining the same, that is, without an increase in the advertising budget or a change in the sales organization, and if competition had no major improvement. I stated this in my letter covering the research report.

Gordon Hughes asked me to come to Minneapolis to present the new packaging program to management and the sales organization. When I stated at the meeting that a sales increase of about 100 percent should be expected from the package change, I was told that management would be satisfied with a 10 percent increase.

About five months after the new Betty Crocker packages were introduced into the market, I met a General Mills executive in a hotel in New York. My wife and I were in the cocktail lounge, having a drink, when a booming voice called out "Louis Cheskin! I wouldn't have imagined seeing you here, just when I'm having troubles brought on by you."

He was in New York trying to get package producers. At this point, the company executives were not ready for an increase in deliveries to the stores. They did not anticipate the demand.

I told him that we should begin taking the packages one step further. I reminded him I had pointed out in discussions that although the logo with the oval gave the Betty Crocker line a family character, the oval lacked symbolism; the line should now have a symbol with favorable connotations. He told me, as others at General Mills have, that the name Betty Crocker provided the symbolism. My reply: the name lacks visual character and has no specific imagery. He said perhaps we should use a Betty Crocker portrait on the package. I said it was worth investigating, but that it was advisable also to consider other devices.

A few weeks later I was advised that a package design firm in New York had been retained to develop a symbol for the Betty Crocker line and that various portraits were being produced of "Betty Crocker."

Al W. Harding, the assistant marketing research director, told me that the New York designers came up with a spoon symbol, but that management did not like it; they wanted to test only portraits, to determine which of them had greatest appeal.

I told him that it would be a great mistake not to test the spoon symbol. I wrote a letter in which I pointed out the danger of making decisions on the basis of a subjective reaction. I urged that General Mills authorize me to test the spoon. In a few days I received the authorization to proceed with the research.

Our tests showed that the spoon had very great strength as a symbol for Betty Crocker products.

The designers were asked to produce packages with the spoon symbol and to improve the appetite appeal of the illustrations. Our research showed that two most vital elements on the food packages were the symbol and the appetite-appeal illustrations.

A few months after the Betty Crocker packages with the spoon symbol and improved cake illustrations appeared on the market, sales had again increased greatly.

Of course, as in the first package change, the brand was supported by a great advertising campaign. The packages were clearly shown in the ads. They made a sharp impression that was retained in the memory and easily recognized in the store.

In two leaps, Betty Crocker gained first position in the market. Before the first package change, the brand was in third position. This was indeed a success story based on a package change. The package became the focal point of the marketing program that led to great success.

4

"MODERN" WHEATIES
FAILS LCA TESTS

WHEN GENERAL MILLS executives saw how great a role the package can play in a marketing program, they asked me to begin work on the breakfast-food line.

The ad agency proposed a program based on "Wheaties have gone modern." They produced a number of package designs to symbolize modernity. I was asked to conduct research to find out whether the "modern" theme would be effective.

We tested the new packages with 1,000 mothers and 200 children. The test results showed clearly that the "modern" concept would not sell Wheaties. Both to the mothers and to the children Wheaties meant "Breakfast of Champions."

The report of December 29, 1954, closed with: "These tests show clearly that the old theme should not be given up. It is advisable to modernize the old concept, but not to go modern.

"I recommend a cleaner figure, brighter and lighter color background, and better readability by redesigning the lettering of the name Wheaties."

On a Saturday when my wife returned from a shopping tour, she said to me, when she saw me standing on the porch sipping a glass of iced tea, "Better sit down, I have something to tell that will shock you." She told me that she had seen in the supermarket the "modernistic" packages of Wheaties that had failed in our tests. This really did shock me. I rushed to the supermarket with my wife to see them. There they were in all their splendor. They were a bright announcement of a marketing disaster, I told my wife.

Monday morning, I called General Mills. I was told by Al Harding, who was then marketing research director, that when top management saw my report, he was told to employ two other marketing research organizations to work on this problem. Both of the other researchers concluded from their "research" that "Modern Wheaties" would be a great success.

The management men had their opinions confirmed. They wanted research that would prove them right and they found it. "Cheskin is not always right," said one executive.

The research director told me he tried to point out that Cheskin does not rely on his own opinion and that his research is reliable and has validation in the market. But he could not support my report because the two other researchers had reputations equal to mine. I told Harding that this Wheaties marketing program was sure to fail.

In a few months the packages had to be withdrawn from the market. Wheaties sustained great injury. (In 1964, ten years later, it was reported in the press that a General Mills executive stated in a speech before a marketing group that motivation research failed to provide the right information for marketing Wheaties. I am reporting this to set the record straight.)

During the Wheaties redesigning episode, Gordon Hughes left General Mills to become research director of Scott Paper Company. Al Harding, the new marketing research director, resigned soon after the Wheaties fiasco.

I regretted the breaking away from General Mills. For a time I felt that I was a member of the General Mills family. I was part of the Betty Crocker success story. But my sorrow did not last long. Procter & Gamble bought Duncan Hines and I was assigned to conduct research on the new packaging program.

Duncan Hines became a great success and was fighting for first position with General Mills. In some markets it achieved, and perhaps still has, the largest share.

5

DAVID OGILVY
INTRODUCES ME TO LEVER
AND TO REED & BARTON

In 1952, David Ogilvy introduced me to Lever Brothers Company. Bob Graustein, director of marketing research, made a strong impression on me. The idea of working with the Lever marketing research department appealed to me.

At Procter & Gamble, I worked with the director of packaging for almost five years before the marketing research department became interested in my service to the company. In the same year (1952) that I met the marketing research director at Lever, I was introduced to the marketing research director at Procter & Gamble. Although I had been having a close relationship with the packaging department and some of the brand managers at P & G, my meeting with and continued contact with the marketing research department was on a formal basis. It appeared to me that the P & G marketing research department considered me competition, rather than an aid to them.

My first assignment from Lever was Good Luck margarine. (Procter & Gamble had no margarine.) On the basis of our first tests, May 2, 1952, I made the following recommendation:

Employ a designer to revise the present package.

1. The four-leaf clover should be given maximum play.

2. The package should be predominantly yellow, not green.

3. The top panel should have an appetite-appeal illustration.

While I was working on Good Luck margarine, I gathered information from our control tests that women like soap in certain colors—pink, aqua, turquoise and yellow. I brought this information to the attention of Procter & Gamble and was told by the P & G marketing research department there was no evidence that "more colors would sell more soap." This released me from my obligation to Procter & Gamble.

I immediately proposed the idea to Lever. I explained to the Lever executives how we get information on color from our "control tests" which are used with every commercial test.

The Lever lab produced soap samples in various shades and tones of pink, aqua, turquoise, and yellow, and asked me to test them to determine which specific colors would have greatest consumer acceptance.

At the same time we tested various proposed package designs for Lux Toilet Soap.

I helped introduce colored Lux; I held press conferences and the Color Research Institute research results were used in news releases to the press. Lux in four colors became a great marketing success. I was told that the sale of Lux more than doubled.

After that, I began to work closely with the Lever MRD personnel on many brands and my connection with P & G was terminated.

I have been working with Lever personnel for over twelve years and my relationship with them has always been pleasant. I have felt part of a team. They know that they can rely on me and I know that I can rely on them. Personally, I have not had even one unpleasant experience with Lever. There have been problems. In more than a dozen years, problems do arise. But we always have solved them easily.

Most Lever executives are men with a broad outlook. Some have subjective tendencies and are opinionated, but as a group, they lean toward objectivity. I have noted that Harold H. Webber, one of the top executives, is interested in the psychosocial aspect of consumers. Lee Pevear, the packaging director, approves of marketing research because, he says, "I am not even a typical consumer." He works very closely with the marketing research department and the brand men. Although my work is with the MRD people, I maintain close contact with Lee Pevear and the brand men.

While I was conducting research on Good Luck margarine and other Lever products, David Ogilvy asked me to conduct research on Reed & Barton sterling flatware. (Ogilvy forgot to confess this in his book *Confessions of An Advertising Man*.) In an illustrated brochure, Reed & Barton gives me credit for the research.

6

PHILIP MORRIS LAUNCHES AN EXPANSION PROGRAM

In 1953, Philip Morris launched an expansion program with great impetus. From the beginning I had a role in the package development program and about a year later LCA and CRI also began to test ad campaigns.

This marketing program involved the creation of new brands of cigarettes, giving new character to old cigarette brands, and diversification by acquisition of new products.

I began to serve Philip Morris a few months after my connection with Lever began. All of the men with whom I worked from the beginning of the expansion program are now in the top positions. I take pride in having worked with them, and I must say I expected that they would achieve their objectives.

George Weissman, who had examined my reports on the Good Luck margarine package at Lever, was appointed special assistant to the president of Philip Morris. (He is now president of Philip Morris, Inc.) His assignment was to conduct studies and evaluate all brands of the company.

Larry Deckinger introduced me to George Weissman. "Philip Morris needs you. The management wants research that encompasses both qualitative and quantitative factors," Deckinger told me.

Weissman said to me: "I read your article in the *Harvard Business Review* and I have seen your research report on

Good Luck margarine. This is the kind of research I want."

My first assignment was to conduct an image study of Philip Morris cigarettes. On the basis of this study, a repackaging program was started. Two package-design houses produced over 100 package designs. These were put through our ocular tests—visibility, readability, and eye movement—and those that passed these tests were put into controlled association tests against the old brown package. The research showed that a new package brought the Philip Morris brand up to date. An effective ad campaign backed its introduction.

Almost immediately following the Philip Morris project, Weissman directed me to conduct research on Marlboro. The objective: to make Marlboro a masculine brand.

I was introduced to Ross R. Millhiser, the new brand manager. (He is now president of Philip Morris, U.S.A.) He turned over to me about thirty package designs to test. Eight that came out with the highest ratings in the ocular measurements were put through association tests. The association tests disclosed, among other things, that logic does not play a major role in marketing cigarettes.

The new Marlboro was going to be a cigarette with a new type of filter; the designer reasoned that an illustration of the cigarette with the new filter on the package would communicate instantly the type of cigarettes the package contained and that this would be an asset. The research showed that it was not nearly as much of an asset as the Philip Morris crest.

The package design with the crest on the front communicated "high quality," whereas the package with the cigarette illustration communicated "ordinary." The package with the crest rated higher than the package with the cigarette illustration in every one of the favorable associations and the cigarettes rated higher in preference.

David G. Lyon, who was the ad agency representative on the Marlboro program says in his book *Off Madison Avenue* (Putnam), "The Marlboro package that went on the market so successfully is almost precisely the same design we had seen in sketch form 18 months earlier," before the research was completed. "It was so outstanding that no research project, no matter how carefully constructed, could louse it up.

"The significance of this story is not the $150,000 which Philip Morris spent on packaging research—such a price would have been cheap had it been instrumental in preventing a mistake or correcting an error."

The directive to the designer came from George Weissman, who was in charge of the program. Ross Millhiser, the brand manager, knew he needed a masculine package, and he had the information that a triangle should serve as the basis for a masculine package. The designer was instructed to produce a number of versions—a variety of treatments.

Because Mr. Lyon does not know what is psychologically significant, he believes that the Marlboro package that went to market is not much different from the design originally submitted by the designer. (I, too, do not know what is psychologically significant; that is why I use research.)

The final package rated much higher in display effectiveness and also in masculine associations which Mr. Lyon wanted or considered desirable.

The triangle is the basic design element in both the original and final package. On request of George Weissman, I sent to Frank Gianninoto "test rated images" showing that a triangle rates higher in masculine associations than any other geometric shape. I also sent to him (and to more than 15,000 others) a reprint from the *Harvard Business Review*, September, 1948, in which I underlined "men preferring angular designs and women curved lines." In addition, Gianninoto received a reprint of my article in *The American Printer*, July, 1948, in which I underlined for him this paragraph: "We found that women like curves and men prefer angles [and I was of the belief until then that men liked curves]." Both articles are reprinted in *How To Predict What People Will Buy* (Liveright).

An illustration in *Secrets of Marketing Success* shows the two first Marlboro package designs we tested, the old package and the final package.

The version of the Marlboro development program Mr. David G. Lyon presents in his book displays his subjectivity. Also, he relies on his memory. I present documentation.

The Parliament cigarettes program followed.

For many years, Parliament was a costly, status brand, in a special box. The objective: to make Parliament a popular brand by changing the package.

Hugh Cullman was the new brand manager. (He is now president of Philip Morris, International.) This time, I decided to avoid waste of time and money on package designing. I outlined a procedure to Cullman:

1. The designer is to produce various logo concepts. We will test these to determine which is the best logo.

2. The designer is to create various symbols. We will test these to find out which symbol is effective with the greatest number of consumers.

3. The designer is to incorporate the logo and the symbol into package prototypes. We will test these to determine their display effectiveness and which of them communicates that Parliament cigarettes are the most desirable cigarettes.

By testing the vital components—logo and symbol—first and then testing only a few complete packages, we cut the cost and saved much time.

One aspect of the research on Parliament, I think, will be of interest. The research disclosed that Parliament cigarettes rated highest in a blue package. The blue packages were put into production for a test market. When Hugh Cullman received the first shipment of Parliament, he was shocked to find that the blue was not clean. It had specks. He called on the phone and asked me what I thought could be done.

On the day Cullman called me, I signed a report for the Consoweld Corporation. The concluding paragraph in this report was that linen is a highly appealing pattern and that a plastic laminate for kitchen counters in a linen pattern would be in great demand. This came to my mind as I talked to Cullman on the phone.

I explained that the unclean effect is caused by dust particles. The tiny particles are not seen on red, but on the deep blue they stick out and make the color appear unclean. I suggested he get packages embossed with a linen texture and we would test them to find out the consumer reactions to such a package. In about three weeks, we received Parliament packages with linen texture and without linen texture.

We conducted a taste-sensation transference test. In part of the test, the participants were asked to smoke a cigarette from each of the packages. The results showed that the cigarette from the package with the linen texture tasted much finer to 80 percent of the participants in the test. The cigarettes in the linen-finish package rated higher in every respect. Of course, both packages contained the same kind of cigarettes.

Other cigarette projects followed. But there is no reason to take space here to tell about them.

However, I think it is worth noting that after testing dozens of ad campaigns and hundreds of ads for Philip Morris, we have found that the best ad campaign upgraded a brand or created a desire to try the brand by about 10 percent; most ad campaigns did little or nothing to promote the sale of a brand of cigarettes, except that the ads kept the brand or package in front of the public. In other words, most cigarette ads do not motivate consumers to buy, but they do show that the brand is available.

Jetson E. Lincoln, who took over George Weissman's responsibilities as Marketing Research Director, when Weissman became Vice President, is now Vice President in charge of finance and planning.

The Philip Morris men who launched the expansion program are now directing the company: George Weissman, President of Philip Morris, Inc., Ross R. Millhiser, President of Philip Morris, USA, Hugh Cullman, President of Philip Morris, International. Joseph F. Cullman, who was president when the company had the greatest growth, is now Chairman of the Board.

7

HOW TO CONDUCT
A MARKETING RESEARCH
SERVICE

IF YOU WANT to conduct store audits and issue sales reports or provide various kinds of statistical information that are of value to businessmen, you will not have many obstacles.

It is, however, not advisable to start your own service until you have had several years' experience working in one of the established marketing research organizations. Academic training does not prepare you for the business world. Academic training is necessary but not sufficient.

Going into business immediately after completing college training has two limitations—lack of experience and lack of evidence of your ability or reliability. Marketing men will not have confidence in you. If you have to earn a living, get a job in one of the established marketing research companies.

If you wish to undertake to predict what people will buy or how people truly feel about new or improved products, packages, symbols, themes, ads, you will find many obstacles.

When I announced that I would conduct motivation research to determine what motivates people in making choices, I was considered an eccentric. Even now, after twenty years, motivation research is still considered by some to be in the realm of the occult.

One remains in business by giving the customer what he wants and needs. If you give him only what he wants, you may be in serious trouble. If you give him only what he needs, he may refuse it.

Frequently, a client wants something he does not need. A

marketing manager wanted me to conduct research to find out which of a number of colors was best for his product. I told him that research was not needed, that we had the information in our files, and that I could give it to him for $100. I did not get him as a client.

He went to a pollster who conducted "research" by asking 1,000 women which of a number of colors they liked best. The majority said they liked the lavender best (they read articles that lavender was in fashion), so the company produced the article for the kitchen in lavender with the result that the product had to be withdrawn from the market. Of course, this convinced the marketing manager that all research was worthless, not that he chose the wrong kind of research.

I have had experience with other marketers who needed research but only wanted my opinion; they would accept my opinion if it coincided with their own.

To be successful in any business, you must give the client both what he wants and needs. If you offer him only what he needs, he may not want it; you have, therefore, to convert his need into a want.

Giving businessmen what they need and want is a basic requirement for success. They need to solve business problems and they want evidence that their marketing decisions are right. But, as I have already stressed, most business men do not know that motivation research can predict what people will buy. Most business executives think psychology is used only in solving clinical problems.

Businessmen are not aware of the progress that has been made in the behavioral sciences and they cannot see how psychology is related to business; they are not aware that modern business deals mostly with psychological factors. Because men in marketing still think in terms of a society of scarcity, they still rely on ways and means that are operative only in marketing necessities for maintaining life; they cannot grasp the essentials that are necessary for selling luxuries, comforts, and status symbols.

Unfortunately, the men teaching in business schools in

most of our universities and colleges have no orientation in the psychological aspect of present-day marketing. Therefore, most of the business-school graduates do not know much more about the psychological factors in marketing than the executives who are nearing retirement age.

Unless you were fortunate enough to attend the Harvard Business School or one of the few other up-to-date schools of business, you have to train yourself for the field of motivation research.

After educating yourself, you have to educate your clients. You have to demonstrate the reliability of motivation research; you have to produce validation. You have to keep on explaining and validating. You have to provide marketing men with a new frame of reference. I still have to explain and validate, after twenty years of rendering the service.

Businessmen are skeptical.

Most of them "think" business success is the result of shrewdness; they have the traditional concept of speculative enterprise.

Many are suspicious of anything new.

Some have had bad experience with the type of research in which verbalisms of consumers were assumed to be equal to behavior of consumers, or research that classified the consumers that were interviewed but did not provide information about consumers' attitudes toward the specific thing—product or package, theme or ad.

Others look upon research as a sales gimmick. They use all sorts of gimmicks; they, therefore, assume that the researcher is selling just another sales gimmick. It is normal for one to use his own yardstick for measuring everything.

After reading this book and my other books, you will have the fundamentals of conducting research on an unconscious level, for determining attitudes, for learning the true feelings of consumers about some specific stimulus—product, package, symbol, theme, ad, etc. You will know the importance of using controls for keeping the test on an unconscious level and for validating the consumer sample.

You should also familiarize yourself with the various schools of psychology and always use the testing tool that will solve the specific problem in the best, most economical, and fastest way.

Guard yourself against becoming fanatical about any one school or kind of psychology. Also, there is danger in assuming that methods and procedures that are operative in measuring abnormal behavior are also effective in predetermining the attitudes of normal men and women.

You must be aware that the psychologist is interested in the person; the marketing researcher should be interested in the stimulus—the product, design, symbol, name, etc. In clinical psychology, the graphic image or word is the means to learn about the person. In marketing research, the person (consumer) is the means of learning about the stimulus—product, design, symbol, name, etc.

You must always be aware that your research must provide both qualitative and quantitative information if it is to have value to your client. It is the only kind of research that can be used as a basis for making a marketing decision.

Although some schools of psychology stress the quantitative aspects and others dwell on the qualitative, you must be aware that life has both quantitative and qualitative aspects, and marketing deals with large numbers of people, with socio-economic classes, and with degrees of product quality.

Do not try to fit the problem to a method, but fit the method to the marketing problem. To be successful in research, you must always remember to be problem-directed.

You must design the test to get the right answer to the problem.

8

HOW I GET
RESEARCH ASSIGNMENTS

THE FIRST TWO YEARS we had men "selling" our services. They were not very successful. For the last eighteen years we have had no one "selling" our services. We have clients who began using our services over a dozen years ago, some twenty years ago.

New clients are brought by my speeches, articles, and books, and through the recommendations of those who have profited from our services; some of these clients are ad agency executives. All presentations of our services are made at our offices, where we can show examples of our research and validate test results of specific marketing programs of well-known brands.

My reputation for making predictions is a great aid in bringing business to LCA–CRI. Few, if any, marketing researchers go on record predicting marketing results. I have never hesitated to make a marketing prediction of share of market for a new or improved product, on the basis of our research evidence on the product, package, and ad campaign.

My predictions of marketing success for Good Luck and Imperial margarine, Dove and Lux soap, Marlboro and Parliament cigarettes, General Electric of Canada light bulbs and Christmas lights, and many other consumer products are well-known.

None of my predictions in the consumer product area, however, produced as much interest as my prediction that the

1961 Lincoln Continental would outsell the 1960 car by over 25 percent, although in 1960, Lincoln had twelve models, and in 1961, it had only two, a sedan and a convertible.

My prediction, in late 1957 and early 1958, that the Edsel, with its huge advertising and promotion campaign, would fail was not believed by most marketing men because they assumed that a campaign as gigantic as that of Edsel could sell anything.

The prediction that the Thunderbird would be a huge success, in spite of the small advertising budget, was not taken seriously by businessmen because they assumed that a new car, particularly an unconventionally styled auto, could not be a marketing success.

But my statements in the press that the 1961 Lincoln Continental would be a success, inspired marketing men to predict that my career as a marketing specialist was about to end.

My declaration that the 1961 Lincoln Continental was mechanically superior to any other American-made car, had styling that rated high in appeal, and had a psychologically potent ad program was not believed by marketing specialists or by admen.

C. H. Dykeman said in *Continental Magazine,* published by the Ford Motor Company, January–February 1962, that "few premarketing research studies have so clearly predicted an outstanding success of a car within weeks of its introduction."

The validation of LCA research has been achieved not only in business but also in the political arena. Predictions on national elections generally become widely known. Mine have been 100 percent accurate and they are on record.

A most dramatic effect was produced by each of these political predictions: In 1948, I predicted that Harry S Truman would be elected, not Thomas Dewey, as the pollsters predicted. In 1960, LCA research showed that John F. Kennedy would be elected by a majority of less than 1 percent. In 1964, I predicted that Lyndon B. Johnson would receive over 60 percent of the votes.

As I said earlier, to stay in business you have to give the client what he needs and wants.

Businessmen do not use marketing research either because they do not know there is such a thing, or because they have no confidence in it, the latter as a result of bad experience with research or of experience with bad research, the kind that does not aid a marketing program, but spoils it, as in the case of Wheaties.

My predictions based on LCA research and their validation by sales results have had wide publicity. Businessmen who keep up with business news and are alert want LCA–CRI research because it provides what they need and want.

I am frequently asked for my opinion. A businessman needs pre-marketing evidence that his new or improved product will be successful or that the marketing tool will be effective. But he wants my opinion because he is accustomed to operate on the basis of opinions and because an opinion costs either nothing or very little and he can get it immediately.

My answer always is that although my opinion is an educated one, it is merely an opinion. An idea of mine is worth testing, but it is not a reliable basis for a marketing program.

I can never win by giving an opinion. If I am right, the man who gets it will conclude that it merely confirmed his own point of view, that I did not tell him anything unknown to him. He will quickly forget that I gave him my judgment. If my advice is followed and it leads to failure, I become the "reason" for the failure in the man's mind. And I can be wrong. I know that my research has never been wrong. But I have frequently been wrong. I do all I can to keep people from confusing my research results with my opinions.

Much of my success is due to the fact that I am interested more in marketing successes than I am in research assignments. I identify myself with the client's problem. His problem is my problem.

While I am occupied with a marketing problem for a company, I do not work for a competitive company. I am completely involved with my client's problem. I contribute all I can to his marketing program.

Among my first clients was an executive who, after hearing me speak, gave me an assignment to conduct a study of his company image. He was delighted with the report that showed his company had a highly favorable image. But when I suggested testing his new package he told me that he had one of the great designers create his line of packages and that one of his new package designs had recently received an award at the packaging show.

In business years, I was only one year old and could not produce validation in the marketplace. I, therefore, undertook to test the prize-winning design on my own initiative, at my own expense. I tested the new package against the old one and against a competitive package with the brand names removed, so that there would not be a brand bias. I conducted a visual (sensation transference) test, and a taste (sensation transference) test, and a brand image (name only) test.

I sent the report to my client with a covering letter in which I stated that I would send him an invoice for this study, if he took advantage of the disclosures in it. If he chose to disregard it, the cost of the study would be my loss, but his loss would be much greater; the study showed that in the new package the brand lost its identity.

The brand did not rate nearly as high when consumers saw the new package as it rated when consumers saw the old package or when they saw the brand name only on a card (in our image study).

The man called me minutes after he received the unsolicited report. He was agitated and told me he wanted an appointment to see me.

In my office, I explained to him that a beautiful design is not necessarily an effective marketing tool. I pointed out to him, and this time he listened, that our research does not disclose whether the package is highly creative or aesthetically stimulating; it discloses whether it communicates to consumers, on both a conscious and unconscious level, the qualities of the product and whether it motivates the consumers to buy it.

"Then high art standards are not marketing standards," he said. "Precisely," I told him.

Although the old package projected a favorable image, although it rated high in favorable associations, the ocular measurements showed that it lacked display effectiveness. Therefore, the designer was assigned to produce new package designs.

The proposed designs were first put through ocular measurements (visibility, readability, eye-movement tests). Those that passed these tests were put into field tests. Within three months there were new packages for the entire line.

In our field tests (controlled association tests), the product in the new packages rated 73 percent in favorable associations and 75 percent in preference; in the old package it rated 27 percent in favorable associations and 25 percent in preference. On the basis of these results, I predicted a sales increase of 100 percent to 200 percent. After four months, the actual sales increase was a little over 200 percent.

Perhaps, one out of a thousand has opportunity forced upon him, and he succeeds in spite of himself. But most of those who are successful seek opportunities or recognize them, and know how to profit from them.

An adman said that he was sure David Ogilvy merely had good luck. "He had nothing many other admen did not have, but he was fortunate to guess right with two or three ideas. Man with the patch on the eye, for example, worked for the Hathaway shirt, but would not work for most other garment companies." He said he knew David Ogilvy well. He insisted that Ogilvy did not understand the psychological implications of the patch on the eye—that he had no concept of the significance of sensation transference.

I do not know David Ogilvy well enough to comment on this. But I do know that many an adman produces a successful ad campaign without knowing why it is successful. He does not understand the psychological factors; he has no grasp of the significance of sensation transference.

However, I, too, have been described as being lucky. Good luck usually comes to those who know how to take advantage of opportunities.

In this book I am presenting ways and means for taking advantage of marketing opportunities.

Opportunities often come from the most unexpected sources. I was once set on the right track by a clerk in our lab.

A label that I thought had all the requirements of a well-designed unit could not pass an eye-movement test. I was puzzled, and none of my associates could explain why this label of a well-known supermarket product could not pass the test. But the clerk who arranged the packages on the shelves for the ocular tests remarked, "Maybe the stars are hard on the eyes; this makes people turn away." Her supervisor disregarded her remark. But she repeated it to me on the phone when she called to give me the results of a second set of tests on this label. I thought she might have pinpointed the trouble. I asked the client to revise the label and eliminate the stars on the background.

The label was sent to us again with only the one change—the stars were eliminated. It passed the test; the eye flow was smooth and it held one's attention.

On another occasion, an error in the test preparation department led to the production of a very effective ad.

A client sent us an ad on which we had to place a photo that we were to receive from an art studio. Our test preparation department placed the illustration below the headline. The ad was excellent as far as eye flow was concerned. Our client again sent the ad to us with a note telling us that we had placed the illustration in the wrong position; it should have been at the upper right of the copy theme (headline). But, in this position, it did not pass the test. The "wrong" ad was right and it was the one that appeared in the print media.

I can understand why marketing and advertising men cannot grasp the significance of sensation transference, because I could not grasp it. I accepted it only after I had seen several tests with hundreds of individuals. I had difficulty accepting it because it was contrary to my frame of reference; it was contradictory to my education; it was in opposition to my orientation. It was a reality I could not face. But without facing it, without accepting it, I would not be able to solve marketing problems.

Without an understanding and complete acceptance of sensation transference, it is not possible to solve problems in marketing psychological satisfactions, that is, in selling design and color, styling and fashion, comfort and status—goods that are not essential for biological survival.

Understanding the psychological implications of sensation transference is, however, not enough, if the researcher is to serve his client as a marketing specialist. He must also have orientation in the graphic arts and in semantics.

Most marketing researchers are not successful as marketing specialists for three reasons:

1. They have no understanding of the full significance of sensation transference and do not recognize ego involvements and defense mechanisms of respondents.

2. They have no orientation in the graphic arts.

3. They have not concentrated on semantics.

Because they lack psychological, aesthetic, and semantic orientation, they cannot design tests that will provide answers to specific marketing or advertising problems and they cannot make recommendations for revision and improvement.

One who does not understand sensation transference cannot suggest using symbols (images or colors) that will provide favorable associations. One who has no orientation in graphics cannot recommend specific graphic alternatives. One who has no mastery over semantics cannot suggest alternatives in copy.

Research statistics in themselves have no significant meaning and do not provide a basis for recommendation.

A researcher who understands the implications of sensation transference can recommend using shapes or colors that may provide the desired associations for the product.

The researcher who has had training in the arts can provide specific graphic alternatives. He can say a circle may be better, let us try it; this kind of blue may have a more favorable association, let us test it, etc.

A researcher who has orientation in semantics can suggest copy like this for an ad: "The man's glass of beer is *half empty* and he wants it filled," instead of merely showing the man's glass *half full,* suggesting to the unconscious mind that the man in the ad could not drink a full glass of this beer.

The marketing researcher does not provide marketing guidance merely by stating that the research shows that the package lacks visibility and the brand name lacks readability, unless he can recommend a design idea or a color that will increase visibility and a typeface or lettering style that will increase readability.

A researcher does not provide advertising guidance merely by stating that the ad does not have smooth eye flow; he should be in a position to recommend a change that may endow the ad with smooth eye flow.

Recommendations are not research evidence but are a basis for a new creative effort that may lead to more effective communication. The revised version has to be put through research for evidence that the revision achieves the intended purpose.

The researcher should use his accumulated knowledge as a basis for forming hypotheses; the researcher's recommendation should provide a basis for the creative person's further effort in creativity.

Research should then be used to determine whether the new creative effort has greater effectiveness.

The research can serve as an idea source for the creative

person as well as evidence of the effectiveness of the graphic and/or semantic communication.

Marketing research is statistical. But in an affluent society, marketing and, therefore, marketing research is not merely statistics. It is psychology; it is graphics; it is semantics.

A letter from a client contained this: "The test we propose, as you see, calls for testing a concept rather than specific patterns. Does this fit your procedures?"

Similar questions have been asked before.

My answer:

A marketing researcher whose orientation is sociology or social anthropology naturally tries to fit a problem to his discipline.

A statistically oriented researcher looks on a problem basically in quantitative terms; his goal is to produce statistics.

A marketing researcher whose orientation is psychoanalysis sees a problem through the eyes of a psychoanalyst.

At Louis Cheskin Associates, we are not married to a specific discipline. We use devices from all disciplines. We design tests to get correct answers.

The methodology is made to fit the problem. We think in both quantitative and qualitative terms. We are statistically and psychologically oriented. We are aware of the psychosocial factors and we occupy ourselves with measurement, not with one discipline.

Also, you should be aware that we will need actual patterns for testing the concept, because consumers react to things, not to concepts, not to ideas. Instead of testing a specific pattern against a control, we will test sets or groups of patterns.

Several times a year we issue a newsletter. Generally, this mailing piece reports marketing successes. Often, the communication is a prediction followed by a report of the fulfillment of the prediction in about four to eight months.

Once each year, a more specific communication is sent out to potential clients; this one spells out the specific services and gives the costs.

TAKE THE GAMBLING OUT OF MARKETING

PRODUCT—We can test your new or improved product before you put it on the market. There are other research organizations that can also do this for you. You should have this done by some reliable organization.

PACKAGE—You will be sure to have a package that sells, if it passes our tests. If it does not pass our tests, Louis Cheskin, our director, with twenty years of phenomenal success, will make specific recommendations for changes.

ADVERTISING—Have it tested by your ad agency, if the agency can conduct research on an unconscious level, research that reveals how consumers react to your product in the ad, not to the ad as a work of art. If the agency cannot conduct this kind of research, we can. We have twenty years of experience and a remarkable record of predicting marketing successes.

PRICE—The right price for the particular market is also predetermined through our research.

For $250 you can determine whether your package has display effectiveness.

For $125 you can find out how readers look at your ad.

For $950 you can find out which of five specific marketing themes or slogans is most effective for a market, or you can learn which of five proposed names is the best for your new product.

Use research that reveals how consumers really feel . . . not what they say.

Our Schedule of Fees with a brief description of our services is enclosed.

We'll send you specific information on request.

The kind of research described above is much less costly than test markets, is reliable, and takes less time. Tests conducted with controls on an unconscious level cannot be ruined by the actions of competitors.

Not even a hundred companies like Louis Cheskin Associates and Color Research Institute could meet the marketing research needs of United States business.

I get research assignments because my research has been validated in the marketplace and clients have confidence in it. The following letters are evidence of this.

Philip Morris presents one of the great success stories in marketing. George Weissman, President of Philip Morris, Inc., wrote:

"I was immensely pleased to learn that you are preparing a book based on your research and marketing activities—and that the Philip Morris case history is to be included.

"The momentum generated during our massive packaging program of 1953 still carries on, although it will be difficult to surpass some of those moments when Marlboro was being introduced. I don't think either of us will ever forget the reaction to the first Marlboro press party when double-talk artist Al Kelly, introduced as a design expert, explained how the Flip-Top box and the package design were selected.

"Lou, our years together have been very productive, and again, I am glad that you are making available your wide experience for use by others."

Quality Bakers Of America Cooperative is a great success story in the food field. Robert L. Schaus, Executive Director, said:

"It seems as if it were yesterday—yet it has been 18 years since I first met with you to further our research efforts for our precious Sunbeam trademark.

"As you so well know we have just completed our fifth major redesign of our entire packaging line without changing even a single hair on Miss Sunbeam's blonde head.

"The continued sales success of our Sunbeam line of breads, rolls, cakes, doughnuts, and sweet goods is unmatched in the baking industry. It certainly testifies to the merits of using good research techniques as an important part of all package design programming.

"Needless to say, we certainly appreciate the important part Color Research has taken in aiding QBA to make each of these major packaging changes successful sales ventures. During these 18 years we have used the services of literally dozens of other research companies to solve many research problems but Color Research is the only research company we have worked with continually during this time.

"It is heartening to know that our new Cameo Package Design has already made a tremendous impression in the marketplace in the changeover from conventional wrapping to the use of polyethylene bags for most of our white breads.

"Once again, we are thankful for the Sunbeam trademark which has made it possible for Sunbeam bakers to meet every challenge or change required by the times. It is a remarkable record when you consider the fact that for over 25 years our Sunbeam bakers have successfully marketed the Sunbeam trademark in its original pictorialization, and yet every other element of our package designs has changed many times.

"Here's looking forward to the challenging future!"

This statement was made by J. V. Cox, Manager-Marketing, General Electric, Canada:

"We are indebted to your research approaches for objective evaluation of many of our major consumer marketing programmes in the light bulb business, and look forward to utilizing your good services in the future."

Robert I. Chien, Director of Marketing Research, G. D. Searle & Co., thought I would appreciate knowing the following:

"Since your study of consumer associations concerning the proposed Metamucil plastic container, we have completed a series of market tests on price and package. I take great pleasure in letting you know that actual sales results showed a statistically significant difference favoring the proposed container over the present at each of the three price levels tested, thus confirming your study.

"A significant number of users also indicated their desire to repurchase Metamucil in the test container."

Benson C. Brainard, President, Lavoptik Company, Inc., said:

"The marketing decisions based on the original group of

tests were right and now the potential is much greater. Our May shipments were the largest for that month in the history of the company."

The Lincoln Continental is a great success story in the automotive field. My predictions based on research that the Lincoln Continental would be a success were not believed by most people. In a letter to me, Herb Fisher, Merchandising Manager, stated:

"Certainly your prediction of success for the Lincoln Continental, made back in 1960, has proved to be most accurate. As you no doubt have read, 1966 Lincoln Continental sales have reached a level never before experienced in the 46 years since a car named Lincoln has been on the market."

The following came from Frank S. O'Donnell, Vice President, Hires Division, Beverages International Inc.:

"Mr. Cheskin, the investment that Hires made in securing your services two years ago continues to reap for us daily benefits and sales as well as the additional bonus of making it easier for us to sell an idea to our customers."

William H. McNamara, General Manager, Blue Star Foods, Inc., wrote:

"Looking through your 20th Anniversary booklet, it occurred to me that I should thank you for your assistance.

"I particularly want to thank you for making it possible for me to attend the seminar you conducted."

(I worked with his father for several years when he was General Manager.)

A. R. Graustein, Jr., Marketing Research Director, Lever Brothers Company, said:

"Consumer research has been challenged and stimulated by your contributions."

To succeed in consumer research or to succeed in any other field, you must challenge and stimulate.

9

PROBLEMS IN THE MARKETING RESEARCH BUSINESS

IN MARKETING RESEARCH, work is relatively easy. Dealing with some clients is difficult. In every field, dealing with people takes more energy than doing the work.

Case histories of my experiences with clients present a picture of what to expect in conducting a service for testing products, brand names, packages, symbols, marketing themes, ads, etc.

I have already made clear that subjectivity still is dominant in business. Scientific methods are not accepted with joy by champions of rugged individualism, by those who still consider private enterprise as gambling, pure risk-taking. To the traditional businessman, marketing is not a science. To him it is an art, an opportunity for self-expression. Profit to him means personal achievement, not a mere material gain.

Business publications stress personal achievement and the risks taken by investors. Few editors of business publications are aware of scientific methodology in marketing.

Industrial production has been revolutionized by electricity. Automation is entering every field. Communication and transportation are changing the ways of everyday life. Most business leaders, however, cling to the methods of business of the nineteenth century.

Although most businessmen are quick to adopt the latest electronic devices for efficient operation, they are incapable of accepting the guidelines of the behavioral sciences; they are not capable of accepting anything that requires that they change their own attitudes and behavior patterns. Most executives can easily accept a new line of merchandise, a new material, a new operations system; they cannot accept a new way of seeing things or any changes in attitude or behavior that they must make. They resist a new frame of reference required for meeting the new conditions in our society.

The most descriptive word for the condition in marketing is chaotic. The transition from an economy of scarcity to an economy of abundance, with demand by consumers for psychologically meaningful goods, has turned the marketing field into a state of confusion.

There are no marketing standards in our highly standardized society. Some marketers insist on making marketing decisions on the basis of hunches. Others ask consumers what they want.

A marketing executive wanted me to interview 10,000 consumers. When I told him that the right kind of test with 1,000 will reveal as much as with 10,000, he could not accept this. He had no concept of sampling. He employed a researcher who interviewed 10,000 consumers.

A producer of a grocery product wanted me to test a "new concept." I told him that consumers naturally react to things, not to concepts, that asking people about concepts can give misleading information. I reported to him a number of failures of marketing programs that were launched on the basis that the concept had been tested. The man employed a researcher who told him that he could test concepts.

Some marketers do not believe in marketing research. Others do not know it exists. Many marketing men say they cannot afford marketing research. Others spend great sums of money on meaningless research. Philco spent $100,000 for interviews of 12,500 consumers: this is $8 per interview. It is not necessary to have such a large sample of consumers, and the cost per respondent is not nearly as great in research that is conducted on an unconscious level and with controls.

Science rules in most production plants; anarchy prevails in most marketing departments.

Most marketing men have no orientation in the behavioral sciences and have not kept up with the psychosocial changes in our society. They, therefore, have no understanding of the procedures necessary for predetermining consumer acceptance of psychologically meaningful products.

Although marketers now deal mostly with psychological needs and wants of consumers, they still think in terms of a society of scarcity, in terms of providing biological necessities —basic commodities—bread, onions, pork.

The drive for personal achievement, with its ego involvement, is dominant in the arena of business. Profit is often considered secondary to personal satisfaction. Subjectivity prevails in many present-day business enterprises.

The president of the Chun King Corporation revealed his subjectivity in the following:

"Jeno Paulucci Tells of 'First Real Bomb' " is the title of an article in the May 13, 1966 issue of *Printers' Ink*. After Mr. Paulucci described some so-called research conducted at an ad agency, he stated: "Finally, I said these guys are all experts so I'll go along with it. With all this research, how could there be much wrong with the package, even if I didn't like what they were showing me?

"Well, when the repackaged Chow Mein frozen line got on the market, it sold products, but not as we had expected. Sales went up 13-15 percent but with the effort that went behind it, it should have gone up at least 30 percent.

"One trouble was that the package was over-researched by the agency. We didn't get a chance to work on it in the marketplace on a test basis. We blindly accepted what the research geniuses said. We didn't challenge them with marketing savvy as we should have." Paulucci concluded that twenty years of packaging has taught him that "research plus intuition are both vital."

I was told by a member of the Chun King organization,

who no longer is with this company, that Mr. Paulucci wants research to confirm his opinion and he added, "He is pretty good on packaging; usually your research confirms his opinion, but not always."

It was difficult for me to take this remark seriously because I thought Mr. Paulucci was a marketing genius, that he was a man of vision, with great initiative. He not only has built a successful company but has been a vital factor in the economic structure of his community. I thought, certainly, he must understand the nature of our research; certainly, he must know the difference between reliable, valid research that determines consumers' true attitudes and research that records consumers' verbalisms. Certainly, he is aware that his subjectivity is not a reliable basis for making a package choice.

Mr. Paulucci's statement about the repackaged Chow Mein frozen line in the *Printers' Ink* article surprised me because our research showed clearly that the package was a weak marketing tool. Here is the LCA report on the basic package for the line (August 27, 1964):

Present Frozen Chow Mein With Chicken Package
(Smiling Woman Holding Plate of Chow Mein—
Yellow Background)

OCULAR MEASUREMENTS

Test		Rating
Visibility		84
Readability—	Chow Mein with Chicken	21
Eye Movement—After considerable hesitation eyes fell on Chun King, moved to woman's face, back to Chun King and left package. Attention was held at each point.		C (Fair)

The visibility of the package as a whole is very good.
Readability of *Chow Mein with Chicken* is extremely poor.
Eye flow and attention-holding are only fair because there is consid-

erable hesitation, and the two most important elements—food illustration and *Chow Mein with Chicken*—get no attention.

The ocular measurements show that the visibility of the package as a whole is misleading. Although the package is seen and has brand identity, it is extremely weak in product identity.

On the basis of these measurements I recommend redesigning.

When I asked why the package was adopted, I was told that management liked it, without being told who, specifically, the management was. The LCA report was disregarded and according to this article, the agency research was accepted. Mr. Paulucci's conclusion is not that he chose the wrong research, but that he did not follow his intuition.

Now, let us note the Chow Mein Mix in a carton for the shelf. We put several proposed packages through ocular measurements. On January 3, 1962, we issued a report on the final phase of the study, a field test of a "practical," rectangular package and a package that "took up too much space" because it didn't have parallel lines and had a handle that was "costly."

Two Chun King Chow Mein Mix Package Designs
Design with Handle vs. Design without Handle

Sample: 200 Housewives   *Area:* Midwest   January 3, 1962

Percent of Favorable and Unfavorable Associations	Design with Handle	Design without Handle
Favorable	82%	18%
Unfavorable	18%	82%
Percent of Preference	Design with Handle	Design without Handle
	85%	15%

The Chow Mein Mix in the package with the handle has 82 percent favorable associations; in the package without the handle it has a rating of 18 percent.

The Chow Mein Mix in the package with the handle has a much larger number of associations with all the favorable attitude terms. It is considered "more expensive" by a large majority of the respondents.

The Chow Mein Mix in the package with the handle rates 85 percent in preference and in the package without the handle it rates 15 percent.

Apparently, this time Mr. Paulucci's "intuition" was in agreement with our research results.

We have researched many products for the Chun King Corporation.

Joseph F. Page, product manager, said in a letter dated August 8, 1960, "Limited, but substantial, exposure to the trade thus far confirms the wisdom of scientific research and we thank you for your competent guidance and service."

Joe Page brought me an assignment to aid his designer in developing a package for a new product—Jeno's Pizza. The letter expressed satisfaction with the guidance my research provided.

Often, the ad agency "contributes" to our research by requesting that we ask some specific questions. The following is a letter I wrote to one agency in order to make sure that the answers to these questions were not confused with responses in a controlled association test:

It should be understood that the questions pertaining to the familiarity of respondents with the multi-pak beer carriers suggested by the agency were asked after the respondents had completed the association test by checking favorable or unfavorable attitude terms with the multi-paks and indicating a preference for one of the six-paks of beer.

The direct questions were asked at the end of the test because such questions cannot be asked in a controlled association test that is conducted on an unconscious level. In this type of test the respondent reveals his attitude toward the package without knowing that we are interested in his reaction to the package.

Frequently, the respondent cannot give correct answers to direct questions about a package because he does not know that he is influenced by the package; he does not give the package much conscious consideration. Also, he often wants to give a prestigious answer or an answer that he thinks gives him status.

The answers, therefore, to the direct questions pertaining to familiarity do not have the degree of accuracy that the responses in the controlled association test have.

Many companies send their packages to Louis Cheskin Associates for testing, but not their ads.

The ads are controlled by the ad agency; admen do not like to submit their creations to us, either, because they feel insecure or because they consider all research an obstacle to creativity. The company management men rely on the agency to handle all phases of ad production.

In order to make a sales prediction, I must know the degree of effectiveness the advertising will have. I insist on testing the advertising, if the client wants a prediction.

First of all, I ask the agency to produce four or five themes. The themes are tested as if they represent actual competitive brands.

Most agencies resist testing themes. The reason they give: The total effect should be tested. My answer: We must have evidence that each major part is effective before determining whether the whole is effective. The theme is the basis for the commercial or ad; it is the foundation; it is the headline and should be the primary point of focus.

Producing the themes does not involve much time and expense, and testing them is less costly than testing a complete commercial for television. For print advertising, if there is research evidence that the theme or headline is effective in communicating and motivating, an eye-movement test is usually sufficient to show whether the ad has attention-getting and attention-holding power.

Almost all the big ad agencies have marketing research departments. Most of the research consists of playbacks and polling; some use so-called depth interviews.

The playbacks are conducted on the assumption that the ad that is remembered by the greatest number of people is the best ad. Those who conduct the research are not aware that most advertising is effective on an unconscious level, that a consumer may be motivated by an ad to try a product, but not be aware that it was the ad that created the desire to buy it.

The pollsters, of course, assume that people will do what they say they will. Sensation transference and defense mechanisms prompted by ego involvement and prestige identification are unknown to pollsters.

Depth interviews are of the clinical variety. They reveal more about the respondent than about the ad. The consumer samples are very small, because depth interviews are costly.

But most admen are not concerned very much about research. They are selling creativity. Their primary concern is to sell to the client, and their basic commodity is creativity, which means (or is supposed to mean) originality.

The assumption is that creativity or originality is in itself the best kind of advertising, not a means for producing effective advertising.

Although admen get lost in creativity and often fail to communicate in a motivating way because they consider creativity an end in itself, they do know a great deal about ad production. Most agencies have art directors who are specialists in graphics; they are oriented in all phases of reproduction processes.

Clients, however, often dictate to the ad agency. One marketing manager of a food product insisted that a newspaper ad announcing a new product should be printed in hi-fi gravure, the sheets of which had to be cut in a way that would mutilate the message.

In roll-fed gravure or rotogravure, fine screens are used, which makes it possible to reproduce fine detail in clear, clean color. But most of these presses have no control for cutting the pages. No matter what the subject is, the cutting of it has to be treated like wallpaper.

For some kinds of ads, roll-fed gravure is an advantage. For example, an ice cream ad showing bricks of strawberry ice cream against a background of strawberries from edge to edge —top to bottom and left to right, no white borders—was very effective. The copy appeared on small white signs against the background of strawberries. It made no difference where the ad was cut off. Nothing could be mutilated. Some strawberries and bricks of ice cream were sliced—a "natural" and "common" effect.

But the marketing man of the food product had his package against a formal background. The rotogravure sheets were cut so that on most of the pages the package illustrations, the brand name, the symbol, and the copy were cut. The ad campaign was a total loss.

One client told me that he did not need our research to aid him in developing effective advertising, because Starch reports showed that his ads had great readership.

We put a number of his ads through eye-movement tests. The instrument showed that some of the respondents, not most, saw his headlines. But they read the copy of other ads on the page.

In the Starch interviews, the respondents said that they read the ads from the prestige store. The eye-movement camera showed that they read the ads of the store that offered bargains.

It is difficult for many marketing men to accept the fact that people cannot tell why they do the things they do.

When the Color Research Institute was only about two years old, a paint company, for which I formulated a color system based on three colorants (primaries), plus white and gray, wanted a special line of barn paint. I told the sales manager that a line of paint for farmers should be researched. He told me that his salesmen were going to do the research under his direction.

When I tried to explain the complexities of marketing research, he told me, "You know a lot about color, but I know how to interview people and my salesmen have been dealing with farmers."

His salesmen asked farmers why they used red barn paint. "Because it is the cheapest paint and lasts a long time," they all said.

He put into his line several earth colors: Green Oxide, Yellow Ochre, and Burnt Umber, in addition to the Red Oxide, and offered the green, yellow, and brown at $1.00 less per gallon than the red. The new line was discontinued because the farmers refused to buy any of the colors, except red, although the cost of the red, which was not better in quality, was $1.00 a gallon more.

Farmers want red because they are oversaturated with green and suffer from "red starvation." Red is complementary to green. It has a physical, physiological, and psychological relationship to green. A farmer cannot be expected to know this.

Farmers want to give the impression that they are practical and economical. Therefore, to a direct question, the answer was that they bought the paint for practical and economical reasons. The actual reason was psychological.

Many marketers have one-track minds and are slaves to the concept of specialization.

Several marketers have come to me for color guidance, but went to pollsters for marketing research on the packages and advertising.

Some, who came to me for marketing research, did not feel confident about my knowledge of color, particularly of the technical aspects.

The marketing executive, to whom I wrote about his "See what they do for your food" campaign, disregarded my advice on the kind of printing plates he should have for his ads and my recommendation to continue using ad campaign based on color.

His reasons: A "color man" told him that a good photograph reproduces all the colors accurately and etching on the engravings is not needed. "If we push color, the sale of white will go down."

Some are not interested in marketing research as a means of getting marketing information, but they are interested in it as a marketing tool.

I encourage my clients to use the research as a selling device. I point out the advantage of showing the buyer at a supermarket chain evidence that consumers will buy this product. The buyer's major interest is for the articles to be taken off the shelves by the shoppers. Evidence that consumer appeal has been predetermined is of great interest to the buyer. Often, this evidence is the reason the buyer places an order.

There are, however, some who want to use research merely as a sales gimmick. They are interested in the word research and in statistical numbers; they are not concerned with accuracy. In fact, they do not care whether the numbers are true or false. Their purpose is to obtain numbers that will put their product in the right light, not to learn whether their product is in the right light, whether it is the kind of product that has appeal to consumers.

One marketing man came to me with a product he said was new and he asked me whether I would aid him in preparing a brochure, showing the prediction that his product would have great appeal.

He pointed out to me that his product was to be sold in three price ranges and then he explained why the three would not be sold at the same price.

I showed him the Schedule of Fees and told him the cost of the study. He asked me to proceed as soon as possible. I told him that we would, that the report would be finished in five to six weeks but that I could give him preliminary figures in about three weeks.

He told me that he could not wait more than a week, that he did not see why I was not able to give him the figures in two or three days.

I explained what it took to design a test with controls and to interview 800 housewives. "You really don't have to interview them," he said to me. "All I want is some good figures and to be able to say that you predict the public will be crazy about it."

"What if the public is not crazy about it?" I asked him. He assured me that he knew that people loved it, that the people in his office liked it, and that all the members of his family liked it. He needed my name, he said, because buyers would not believe him.

In a similar experience in the past, I blew my top. This time, I controlled myself. I told him with as much self-control as I could muster that I make predictions on the basis of facts. By testing with the right sample of consumers, I can predict how all potential consumers will react. My personal opinion may or may not be in agreement with the consumer reactions.

He told me he had a huge sales force. I pointed out that a consumer may buy something new to try it. If she does not like it, she will not buy it again. "I only want each customer to buy one," he said. A year later he will have something new, he told me. He did not think I was cooperative.

In the question period following a speech, I was asked, "Have you ever been wrong?" I answered that I am often wrong, but my research is never wrong. I offered to write a check of $1,000 to anyone who could show evidence that a prediction I made on the basis of my research was wrong.

A man raised his hand. The audience coaxed him to accept my invitation to come up to the stage and tell about "the failure of my prediction."

On the stage, he said in an agitated manner: "We sent a can of ham to Louis Cheskin Associates for tests. Mr. Cheskin said in his report that the brand name had poor readability and that the label did not get and hold attention. He recommended changes. We made all the changes, but the label did not increase sales."

I asked the man, "What else did the research report say?"

He said he did not remember. I then asked: "Did it say that my recommendation is not the same as research evidence, that new label designs had to be produced and sent to us for tests to determine whether my recommendations prove to be right or whether your designer's interpretation of my recommendations is as I visualized them?" The man said: "Oh yes, I remember, but we couldn't send in the new labels. We just did what we thought you wanted."

There was great laughter. When it subsided, I explained to the audience that this was not all that the report had said. It also said that if the ocular-measurements instrument tests showed the label design had display effectiveness, it had to be submitted to a field test, with a sample of several hundred consumers, to determine how the label rated psychologically, whether it had the high-quality connotations in keeping with the high price, whether it communicated high quality and promoted a desire for the product.

Why did this man say that our research had failed when he was aware that he did not follow through with the research? Why did he merely take the first step?

There are several psychological implications in this. A major factor is the desire to use research as a sales gimmick, not as a means of getting information on the effectiveness of the label as a marketing tool.

The man had no interest in research; he merely wanted to be in a position to say to his customer that the label was produced on the basis of Louis Cheskin Associates research.

He resented having to use research as a sales tool to begin with; when it failed him, he actually became hostile to Louis Cheskin Associates. He showed the hostility when he volunteered to show that the research failed. He also revealed greed. Because of his hostility and greed, he failed to realize that the $1,000 check was a mirage. He lost his sense of reality and sense of awareness that he could not show that the research had failed, that he would actually show that he had failed.

On another occasion, following my speech to an audience of marketing men, a dignified-looking old gentleman stated that he thought research was bunk, that he had used it twice and each time it brought him great losses. Obviously, the man was hostile. He said he wanted the audience to know the other side of marketing research—the failing side. "In theory, research sounds all right but not in practice," he told the audience.

"What kind of research have you used?" I asked. "Was it polling, depth interviews?" He repeated, "It was research, it was marketing research, and it made me lose money." I asked, "Was it the kind of research I just described?" He thundered, "What's the difference, it was called marketing research."

This man, president of a major company, was recently retired. I do not know what the new president thinks of research. But there are many companies in the United States with presidents who are hostile to marketing research, mainly, although not wholly, because they resent the new marketing conditions that require research. They still "think" in terms of a society of scarcity.

Some marketers wanted me to save their businesses or to help them make fortunes. But they were concerned about my using their marketing programs for promoting research.

One executive came to me when his product was almost completely replaced on supermarket shelves by competition. I told him without reservation that I knew how to give his product new life in the market. I assured him that with an investment of about $5,000 or $6,000 in research and a few thousand for development, his product would again become an important commodity in the supermarket.

I aided him in modernizing the product, developing an effective package, creating a motivating ad, and producing a promotion brochure with research documentation.

When I told him I wanted several thousand copies of the ad to mail out with a letter, at our expense, explaining the new product to the public, the trade, and press, he told me that he did not have a budget for additional printing. I managed to get promotion for his new product and he became a success in spite of the limitations he put on himself.

There are times when a client has to be forced to do the right thing. When clients want to use me or my research for promotion purposes, and they often do, they give me the right to insist that they carry out the marketing program in accordance with the research disclosures.

Whenever I see a client deviate, I write a letter stating that under no circumstances is my name to be used in connection with this program, and that I am going on record that I do not approve of it and that it was not based on our research. This has kept many an executive from disaster by making a decision on a subjective basis.

Generally, executives who disregard the research results do not understand the research. They are the men who say, "Cheskin says," not that "Cheskin research shows." One who says, "Cheskin says" is just as likely to say "X and Y say Cheskin is wrong." Then he feels he is being rational and logical by following the "opinion" of two instead of one man. The entire matter is kept on a subjective level. The focal point is not on the problem and the means for solving it, but on the personalities.

Men who are not involved with personalities, but are truly interested in research, may be limited by their frame of reference. Some insist they want only the field tests; the large numbers of interviews are considered magic. Others want only the ocular measurements; they think that only instruments can be objective.

I have to explain that each kind of measurement has limitations. The ocular measurements reveal the display characteristics of the package, but do not reveal the viewers' attitudes. The controlled association test reveals the consumers' attitudes, but does not show how effective the package is in attracting attention.

Often, when a marketing man hears me use the word "limitation," he is surprised, or disappointed. "I didn't think your research had any limitations," said one businessman to me. I explained: The total research has no limitations, but each phase of the research is limited in the kind of information it provides.

Often, when a traditional businessman discovers marketing research, he behaves like a man getting religion; he expects a panacea.

Some marketers think my analysis is the most vital part of a Louis Cheskin Associates report. When they send in assignments, they state that they want me to make an analysis of their problems—new product, brand name, package, ad, etc. They reveal a lack of awareness that my analysis is actually a summarization and interpretation of the test results.

Others believe that the percentage of total favorable associations and percentage of preference reveal everything. One man was surprised to find in my recommendation that one association was more motivating than all the others.

The percentage of total favorable associations showed that design B was the best. But in appropriateness for a bathroom, design C rated considerably higher.

Another marketer was disappointed because the container that rated very high as "attractive" and "beautiful" rated very low as "practical." The fact that it was not practical made it undesirable, although in total favorable associations, in psychological or aesthetic appeal, it rated very high.

Frequently, research shows that consumers are ambivalent; they "love" something for one reason, and "hate" it for another. The businessman then has to find something that is closer to neutral, that people do not love so much and do not hate.

Many executives are disappointed when research reports show that they have been wrong. And a considerable number refuse to accept the research results.

In some corporations I have become unpopular because I took a definite stand. In one company, the chief executive dislikes me intensely because when he was the No. 2 man, he was against carrying out a program that my research showed would be a success. On the basis of my report, the program was adopted and became a great success. When he became senior executive, he discontinued the Louis Cheskin Associates service. When asked whether I was doing research for him, he answered, "Cheskin had a streak of luck. That does not mean he would have it again; we are doing all right without him." He was recently retired, and I am again doing research for that company.

Subjectivity often is an obstacle in problem-solving; the ego often dominates the problem. The ego-dominated executive wants a problem handled so that it is associated with him; solving the problem is secondary to who solves it or how it is solved.

We can change things much more easily than we can change ourselves. Most people are not even aware that there is ever any reason for changing their attitudes and behavior.

Generally, when the executive with whom I deal leaves the company, I lose the account. The new man wants everything new. He wants to choose his own research. He makes his contribution by making changes. But the man who had been using my services and knows them well takes Louis Cheskin Associates research to his new position.

Those who have been practicing marketing research in the traditional manner—pollsters in particular—are most antagonistic to all motivation research.

I have been making predictions on the basis of controlled tests for over twenty years.

My accurate predictions are a matter of record. To date, each one was correct.

But I have had to present evidence of this to each business executive with whom I have discussed LCA research, to convince him that testing on an unconscious level has validation in the marketplace.

10

"GREAT OPPORTUNITIES"
I REJECTED

MARKETING EXECUTIVES who understand controlled consumer motivation research are few.

Those who have been using controlled consumer motivation research, of course, know its value. There are some who have not used it but have observed its role in many marketing successes.

Some business leaders fully understand the potential of valid motivation research and they put forth every effort to make it their monopoly.

In 1958, "a deal" was offered to me by one of America's largest corporations. This chemical company had spent a year making a study of LCA–CRI methods and procedures. A proposal was made to me by this company to provide us with all the work we could process. It was suggested that we increase our capacity to some extent and that we would not have to be concerned about research projects. This company would keep us busy.

The financial arrangement was very tempting, but it meant that we would be taken over and owned by the chemical company; we would lose our identity. After much contemplation and discussion with my associates, I rejected the proposal.

The same year, the marketing research director of another company suggested that LCA–CRI do all the marketing research for his company. It meant 70 percent of our capacity would be devoted to one client. Without discussing this with any of my associates, I rejected the account, because I thought that it meant putting most of our eggs into one basket.

In 1962, an attorney I know socially suggested in a casual conversation that LCA should be made a public property. I did not take it seriously and did not grasp what it meant. Less than six months later, I was contacted by a financing company which offered to make LCA a public property. The meaning of this was explained to me in great detail. It was a grandiose plan. It staggered the imagination.

Instead of discussing this proposal with my entire staff, I thought I should discuss it with my wife. We considered this proposal with great solemnity. After having thought deeply for almost an hour, my wife spoke up:

"This program would kill you. I don't want to be a rich widow. I want you to begin to cut down, not to expand. Now, you should begin to let the young men carry the burden. You should run the organization without killing yourself. An expansion program would shorten your life." Never before had Vivian been in such a serious mood. On the following day, I rejected the proposal.

About five years ago, a well-known newspaperman introduced me to a noted lawyer who wanted me to help him set up a "motivation research organization for studying management-labor problems." I agreed to serve as a consultant. The journalist was to play a management role; a specialist in the behavioral sciences was recruited to direct the program. Offices were rented across the street from mine. Within a month there was an institute with a staff of academicians and theoreticians with various orientations. All of them were recognized specialists in the behavioral sciences.

The sponsor and backer, for whom the institute was named, had some specific problems—basic questions to which he sought answers. The institute could not get started getting answers to specific questions because it had many generals who did not agree on procedure, and no soldiers.

I was asked to solve the problems presented by the sponsor

of the institute. We conducted three studies to get answers to the three most important questions. All three were vital socio-economic and psychosocial problems. The institute's sponsor-backer was delighted with the reports.

A week after he received the reports of the three studies, the institute's sponsor introduced me to a man who was interested in Cuba. I was asked to conduct an extensive study of Cuba. Fidel Castro and his "band" were in the mountains.

Some of the vital questions the Cuban wanted answered were: How did the Cuban peasants feel about Castro? What were the attitudes of the low-income urban dwellers? What did the educated Cubans think of Castro?

While the tests were being designed for Cuba by my staff, the institute group of men were talking about it. The sponsor invited me to his apartment for dinner and told me that he was discouraged; he did not think that the people of the institute would get going with anything practical. He wanted me to take over.

I explained to him that it was impossible, that I had my hands full with my own organization. "Then if you can't direct it, I want you to be the heir and I want to delegate my authority to you. It means you will have my responsibility of establishing policy and managing the financial affairs. But you need not actually direct the activities." He said all this to me as if he were in a hurry and added, "I have not been feeling well lately."

The same evening he also urged me to go to Cuba. I told him that I would, after the tests were ready to go into the field in Cuba. We were planning to have about 20,000 interviews in three socio-economic classifications. I wanted personally to check the field samples (percentages of peasants, city workers, professionals).

Legal papers were prepared giving me full authority over the institute and making me the heir to everything related to it. The institute sponsor, the lawyer who prepared the document, and I had lunch, and the document was presented to me for approval. I approved, on condition that the document be signed after the directors of the institute were informed of this. I thought that they, or some of them, might object to my having veto power.

They certainly did object. It was made clear to them that their incomes would not be affected, that their positions would not be changed in any way. But they expressed a definite objection to my veto power.

It was decided to discuss this matter again a week later. I delayed signing the document. Meanwhile, the sponsor was going to his farm to take a rest.

He never returned. He fell ill and died. The study on Cuba was never carried out (Castro took over a few months later). The "institute" was closed. But I will always remember the old man. He was a delightful person.

It would have been a great mistake for LCA to have gone public, and it would have been disastrous for me to have accepted the responsibility of directing the "institute," with personnel not of my choosing and with many sorts of involvements which I would have inherited.

I was asked how it feels to have a pioneering enterprise twenty years old and what I remember most of the birth of LCA–CRI.

After twenty years, I still remember the reaction to my statement, in a speech before a group of marketers, that my organization was going to conduct marketing research on an unconscious level. "Are you going to knock the people you interview to unconsciousness before you interview them?" asked one member of the audience.

I explained that "unconscious level" meant that the respondent was unaware that we are testing the container or ad, not the product. I pointed out that the person is not aware that he is motivated by a package or advertisement; therefore, in order to find out how he reacts to the brand or product in the package or ad, we must not assign any importance to the container or ad. I explained sensation transference from the package to the contents, from the ad to the product in the ad. I stressed that consciously, we buy products that satisfy rational wants, but unconsciously, we buy packages, styling, design, color, to satisfy wants that are emotionally inspired. I told the audience that people buy psychological satisfactions, but in a direct interview they will tell you that they buy things to fulfill practical needs. This is why direct questions do not get true answers, and we must test on an unconscious level in order to learn whether the package or ad communicates the character and quality of the product. Although this may be very basic and understandable to many marketers now, it was almost completely incomprehensible to my audience in October, 1945.

My explanation received no applause. In fact, my speech was not applauded. My associate, who was in the audience, was discouraged. I was not. I knew it would take time for the basic idea of sensation transference to become widely understood.

A year later, I addressed an advertising group. I stressed in my speech that the essence of advertising is motivating communication, that unless an ad is effective in its communication semantically and graphically, it does not sell merchandise. Creativity, I said, is a means for producing effective advertising, it is not an end; the copywriter and graphic artist should strive, not to express themselves, but to communicate and motivate.

My speech was met with silence. I did not reach my audience, but I was not discouraged. I knew I would have to write many articles and books on communication versus self-expression in advertising, as well as on packaging as a marketing tool, not as a work of art, before the ideas would be grasped.

The birth pangs of CRI research lasted almost three years. The article "Indirect Approach to Market Reactions" in the *Harvard Business Review*, September, 1948, introduced our research into the marketing arena. In 1947, we were already serving some large companies—Procter & Gamble, Standard Oil—but not until the close of 1948, after the article appeared, did our services have wide acceptance.

The cold reception of my first two speeches, I remember well. But I also remember the warm reception of the article.

I succeeded in business by guarding myself against subjectivity, by not permitting my personal opinion to show itself in any research tests plan or research analysis.

Frequently, I have signed a report in which I recommended marketing a product that I personally disliked. Just as often, I think, I have pointed out that a product had no chance of success, although it appealed to me personally.

Without objectivity, there is no research and in marketing (in an affluent society) consumer attitudes and product acceptance can be determined by testing on an unconscious level.

My success in marketing research is based on discovering sensation transference in the marketplace, on conducting research on an unconscious level with controls, and in maintaining complete objectivity.

My orientation in psychology, graphics, and semantics, and the fact that I make specific recommendations on the basis of the research results are of value to my clients.

The "great opportunities" that were offered to me were opportunities for bigness, for great wealth, perhaps.

I rejected them because my idea of success is to have a high standard of living with good health and with the time and opportunity to enjoy the arts and to participate in the social and cultural activities in the community.

I have reached my goal. Now, I merely want to retain it.

11

STUDIES OF MEDIA

MARSHALL MCLUHAN says: "The medium is the message." He says that our mass communication media, reaching people in all parts of the earth, are producing a new human environment. The electric medium reaches the literate and the illiterate. All people in the world now live in the utmost proximity, involved in one another's lives by electric technology. Soon, we will all be members of one tribe. The common language, electric communication—television, radio—unifies all peoples, members of all cultures, the educated (in traditional culture) and the uneducated. The earth will be one village.

In this book, we are concerned with specific messages, about specific products, for specific classes of consumers.

Some marketing researchers are almost completely immersed in classes. "You are what you do," says one.

Others seek Freudian symbolism in all situations. "All women have the same basic urges," says the best-known Freudian in the business arena.

I am not married to any specific discipline, but I know that sampling of consumers must be based on classes and I know that in many marketing situations there are Freudian implications.

Studies of media show that the message, to be effective, has to be created for the specific audience, and the medium has an effect on the message. A communication does not have the same effect on television, on radio, and in print.

Frequently, I am asked which of the advertising media is the most effective. This is not a realistic question, because it is based on the assumption that all products can be sold in the same way or that one medium is best for all products.

We have clear evidence that one medium is best for one type of product, another medium for another type. Also, one medium shows one side or one aspect of the product; another medium shows another aspect. This means that it is advisable to use more than one medium.

Our files contain considerable evidence that the print media—newspapers and magazines—are generally much more effective in selling food, home furnishings, and wearing apparel. But, there are exceptions to this. For example, we found that TV is, in some cases, more effective in selling beer.

An analysis of a number of ad campaigns shows clearly that the type of theme or specific appeal is a factor. One theme or appeal often fits one medium better than another.

If the emphasis is on appetite appeal, the print media are best. If the emphasis is on fun in action or where sports are involved, television is best. If the slogan is particularly catchy, radio is best.

Meat, we found, has the greatest appeal in color printing. The appetite appeal proved to be a more vital factor than any theme or slogan.

An analysis of ad campaigns for wearing apparel reveals that if a garment has a single new benefit that can be demonstrated in action, TV is an effective medium. But if the garment has more than one benefit, or if it is not a benefit derived from some completely new material, or if it is not easy to demonstrate, print media are much more effective.

The advantage of the print media—newspapers, magazines —is that the reader can absorb the message at his own pace. A commercial on TV may be too fast for one consumer to grasp and annoyingly slow for another type of consumer.

In radio advertising, also, the timing must be the same for all listeners.

We have found that people like to study ads of home furnishings and of wearing apparel; they are irritated and antagonized by a TV commercial because it denies the individual the opportunity to study the ad.

The print media—newspapers and magazines—are, with few exceptions, the most effective for selling home furnishings and wearing apparel because they make it possible for the individual to view the ad in a leisurely fashion.

Our studies show that TV has the greatest impact. But the print media rate much higher in favorable associations and have much greater believability.

The print media—newspapers, magazines—reach people through one of the senses, the eyes.

Radio reaches people through one of the senses, the ears.

Television reaches people through both the eyes and the ears. This is the major reason why television has greater impact than any of the other media.

However, impact does not mean favorable effect. Impact is not the same as motivating power.

Example: A study of advertising of a line of packaged meats in two media—color printing and television—showed that the color printing was much more effective. It motivated almost twice as many consumers to try the brand. Why? Because color has great psychological appeal. Color has appetite appeal. Color motivates consumers. Although the effect of color printing reaches consumers through only one of the senses, it is a very powerful effect.

What can color television contribute to advertising? Color can do for television what it does for printing. And combined with effective sound, color television can be very powerful indeed. It can be overwhelming.

In color television the theme is still the base. The graphics must be built around the theme.

People are affected by the total commercial—music, words, imagery, color—but they can repeat only the theme.

The graphic, realistic effect of a potent commercial produces a feeling or experience that remains in the subconscious mind; the words, however, remain on a conscious level. They are remembered and can be passed on to others.

If the graphics with color do not produce an emotional effect, the words will not be remembered. Poor graphics or bad color detract from the verbal message; effective graphics and color endow the verbal message with great power to motivate consumers.

Effective sound means music as well as words, perhaps music more than words. Music, like color, reaches the emotions. The combined effect of the right color and appropriate music cannot be achieved with any combination of words.

A realistic scene, which means a scene in natural color, is not a picture of reality; it is reality.

A radio commercial says this is a delicious, cold, thirst-quenching drink.

The commercial on television says this is a delicious, cold, thirst-quenching drink, and you can see in black and white the cold beverage taken out of the refrigerator; you can hear the crackling of the ice cubes.

On color television, the commercial says this is a delicious, cold, thirst-quenching drink, and you can see in full or natural color the cold beverage taken out of the refrigerator; you can hear the crackling of the ice cubes.

Which of the three commericals is the most effective? Here is how they rate:

The theme, that is, the words, rated 65 percent in favorable associations and 46 percent in preference (for the product).

In black and white, that is, the same theme with the support of black and white graphics (photography) rated 69 percent in favorable associations and 53 percent in preference.

The same theme rated 88 percent in favorable associations and 85 percent in preference (for the product) when it was presented in full or natural color.

Specifically, this means that the same words with illustration in black and white were a little more effective than words alone; with illustration in color they were almost twice as effective.

Not only the words, but also the sound, the music, is more effective when the message is presented in full or natural color.

Hearing the word "cold" is not the same as feeling cold. Hearing the word "hot" is not the same as feeling heat. Being told that something is beautiful is not the same as seeing beauty. Color can make you feel cold. Color can make you feel heat. Beauty is color as well as form.

Color has great power because it causes viewer involvement. Color vibrates and it draws the viewer into the scene. Color, the right color, that is, reaches the emotions and involves them.

When color film was made available to amateur photographers, the number of amateur photographers multiplied greatly.

Color television has tremendous potential as a medium. But how this medium is used is another matter.

Trite commercials in color will not merely annoy; they will antagonize.

Mediocre graphics will not merely be disregarded; they will alienate consumers.

There are, of course, very many technical problems. But these problems will soon be solved.

More difficult to eradicate from television advertising will be the purely subjective commercials that fail to communicate, the offensive commercials and the irritating ones.

Right color is real color. The real is believable. The viewer is not afraid to become involved with the real, with reality that promises pleasure.

Psychological devices or controlled motivation research methods will have to be used to determine whether the color is "right" or "wrong." Polling or direct interviewing will not produce the right answers.

To direct questions, men and women try to give rational answers. Because they are not aware that they are affected by the color, they attribute their reactions to some "rational" aspect associated with the color.

Many studies show that food in the "wrong" color is rejected. When asked about it, the respondent does not say he does not like the color of the food; he says he does not like the food or he says it does not taste good.

Color television certainly presents problems. But it also presents a great challenge and a tremendous potential for motivating consumers.

However, radio has some advantages that color television does not have. One can listen while working or driving a car. Radio permits the listener's imagination to build images in his mind. Television leaves little or nothing to the imagination. Television is very graphic and specific. In color, television is most convincing and highly motivating, but it provides no opportunity for the imagination.

Color television can present "reality" that is believable. Radio can present ideas that the listener can build into images—subjective images that are emotion-laden.

When Orson Welles announced on the radio that the Martians were attacking our planet, millions of people became aroused. The announcement created frenzy. Such emotion-rousing is not possible in any other medium.

A dramatic announcement in the print media is more emotion-rousing than on television, because the printed word permits the imagination to build images. However, the image-building potential of a printed message is not as great as that of radio. The reader can contemplate and analyze a printed message; he reacts instantly to a radio message.

The voice can have emotion-producing power. A dramatic message in a dramatic voice can have an overwhelming effect.

To the question of which medium to use, my answer always is that it depends on your message, or what you are communicating.

Nine studies on communication media (in 1957, 1960, 1961, 1962, 1963, 1964, 1965, 1966, 1967) show attitudes toward advertising in five media. One of the studies is reproduced here.

ASSOCIATION TEST: Attitudes toward Five Communication Media

Sample: 5919 (Total)

The study, conducted in January, 1964, reveals attitudes toward advertising in the five communication media—television, radio, newspapers, magazines, and billboards.

PERCENTAGE OF FAVORABLE ASSOCIATIONS AND IMPACT
Newspaper advertising has the highest percentage of favorable associations (81 percent) and is second in impact (total number of responses).
Magazine advertising has the second highest percentage of favorable associations (70 percent) and is lowest in impact.
Television advertising has the third highest percentage of favorable associations (53 percent) and has the greatest impact.
Radio advertising has the fourth highest percentage of favorable associations (39 percent) and is third in impact.
Billboard advertising has the lowest percentage of favorable associations (21 percent) and is fourth in impact.

ASSOCIATIONS WITH SPECIFIC ATTITUDE TERMS
Among both men and women, newspaper advertising has the largest number of associations with "true," "informative," "sincere," "beneficial," "honest," and "important."
Television advertising has the largest number of associations with "pleasing" and "like best," also with "false," "irritating," "insincere," "in bad taste," and "deceptive."
Billboard advertising has the largest number of associations with "not informative," "not beneficial," "not important," and "like least."
Newspaper advertising is considered "more for men" and television advertising is considered "more for women."

Each year the five communication media have maintained their relative positions in percentage of favorable associations, with one slight difference since 1960. In 1961, magazine advertising had 2 more percentage points than did newspaper advertising in favorable associations.

Of the five communication media, TV has the greatest impact. This should not be disregarded because it means that the public has great interest in TV. But, the fact that the attitudes toward advertising on TV are highly unfavorable should be given careful scrutiny by those who spend great sums of money on TV advertising.

The fact that the print media have greater believability means that, although they do not attract as much attention as TV, they can serve as a vehicle for motivating consumers more effectively.

Also, there are indications that there are more irritating commercials on TV than there are irritating ads in the print media.

Table 5 shows that TV has not regained the favorable associations (84 percent) it had in 1957.

TABLE 1

Number and Percentage of Favorable and Unfavorable Associations

Television

	Number of Associations		Percentage of Associations	
	Favorable	Unfavorable	Favorable	Unfavorable
2,820 Men	9,979	8,450	54	46
3,099 Women	11,201	9,975	53	47
5,919 Total	21,180	18,425	53	47

Radio

	Number of Associations		Percentage of Associations	
	Favorable	Unfavorable	Favorable	Unfavorable
2,820 Men	5,839	7,159	45	55
3,099 Women	4,404	9,029	33	67
5,919 Total	10,243	16,188	39	61

Newspaper

	Number of Associations		Percentage of Associations	
	Favorable	Unfavorable	Favorable	Unfavorable
2,820 Men	11,929	2,830	81	19
3,099 Women	12,866	3,060	81	19
5,919 Total	24,795	5,890	81	19

Magazine

	Number of Associations		Percentage of Associations	
	Favorable	Unfavorable	Favorable	Unfavorable
2,820 Men	7,877	3,575	69	31
3,099 Women	9,746	3,904	71	29
5,919 Total	17,623	7,479	70	30

Billboard

	Number of Associations		Percentage of Associations	
	Favorable	Unfavorable	Favorable	Unfavorable
2,820 Men	3,173	9,848	24	76
3,099 Women	2,279	10,261	18	82
5,919 Total	5,452	20,109	21	79

TABLE 2

Number of Associations—Total
Sample: 5919 (Total)

Favorable	TV	Radio	Newspaper	Magazine	Billboard
True	2,330	1,323	2,742	2,005	770
Pleasing	2,513	1,053	2,332	2,093	758
Informative	2,526	1,247	3,019	1,866	632
Sincere	2,036	1,072	2,618	1,954	593
In good taste	2,088	1,085	2,696	2,237	718
Beneficial	2,668	1,217	3,088	1,896	570
Honest	1,774	977	2,820	1,909	592
Important	2,686	1,296	3,343	1,757	504
Like best	2,559	973	2,137	1,906	315
Total	21,180	10,243	24,795	17,623	5,452
Unfavorable					
False	2,284	1,773	816	881	1,803
Irritating	2,547	2,002	685	715	1,822
Not informative	1,464	1,735	608	952	2,742
Insincere	2,459	1,904	809	861	1,896
In bad taste	2,267	1,804	642	856	2,077
Not beneficial	1,563	1,778	557	869	2,747
Deceptive	2,721	1,902	857	879	1,765
Not important	1,418	1,675	499	897	2,933
Like least	1,702	1,615	417	569	2,324
Total	18,425	16,188	5,890	7,479	20,109
Unclassified					
More for men	2,176	1,192	3,060	1,245	751
More for women	3,333	905	1,203	2,341	273
Grand total	45,114	28,528	34,948	28,688	26,585

TABLE 3

Number of Associations—Men
Sample: 2820 (Men)

Favorable	TV	Radio	Newspaper	Magazine	Billboard
True	1,098	731	1,340	941	468
Pleasing	1,215	601	1,140	914	415
Informative	1,195	697	1,470	871	353
Sincere	938	618	1,268	890	354
In good taste	1,014	655	1,311	966	406
Beneficial	1,238	688	1,435	858	337
Honest	802	582	1,327	843	344
Important	1,253	733	1,584	806	304
Like best	1,226	534	1,054	788	192
Total	9,979	5,839	11,929	7,877	3,173
Unfavorable					
False	1,054	808	385	409	892
Irritating	1,143	918	326	364	872
Not informative	701	752	297	488	1,322
Insincere	1,130	878	388	393	933
In bad taste	1,040	754	311	420	1,011
Not beneficial	716	790	271	386	1,332
Deceptive	1,277	814	412	399	904
Not important	661	757	234	426	1,396
Like least	728	688	206	290	1,186
Total	8,450	7,159	2,830	3,575	9,848
Unclassified					
More for men	1,084	551	1,344	650	326
More for women	1,632	450	490	1,035	101
Grand total	21,145	13,999	16,593	13,137	13,448

TABLE 4

Number of Associations—Women
Sample: 3099 (Women)

Favorable	TV	Radio	Newspaper	Magazine	Billboard
True	1,232	592	1,402	1,064	302
Pleasing	1,298	452	1,192	1,179	343
Informative	1,331	550	1,549	995	279
Sincere	1,098	454	1,350	1,064	239
In good taste	1,074	430	1,385	1,271	312
Beneficial	1,430	529	1,653	1,038	233
Honest	972	395	1,493	1,066	248
Important	1,433	563	1,759	951	200
Like best	1,333	439	1,083	1,118	123
Total	11,201	4,404	12,866	9,746	2,279
Unfavorable					
False	1,230	965	431	472	911
Irritating	1,404	1,084	359	351	950
Not informative	763	983	311	464	1,420
Insincere	1,329	1,026	421	468	963
In bad taste	1,227	1,050	331	436	1,066
Not beneficial	847	988	286	483	1,415
Deceptive	1,444	1,088	445	480	861
Not important	757	918	265	471	1,537
Like least	974	927	211	279	1,138
Total	9,975	9,029	3,060	3,904	10,261
Unclassified					
More for men	1,092	641	1,716	595	425
More for women	1,701	455	713	1,306	172
Grand total	23,969	14,529	18,355	15,551	13,137

TABLE 5

**Summary: Percentage of Favorable Associations
With Advertising in Five Communication Media**

Year	Media				
January 1957	TV	Radio	Newspaper	Magazine	Billboard
Men	82	20	55	50	38
Women	86	17	63	57	18
January 1960					
Men	47	36	81	74	39
Women	51	32	85	78	24
January 1961					
Men	57	35	69	68	25
Women	54	28	78	82	14
January 1962					
Men	56	45	77	66	18
Women	57	44	77	70	18
January 1963					
Men	50	35	80	62	29
Women	59	33	74	74	18
January 1964					
Men	54	45	81	69	24
Women	53	33	81	71	18
January 1965					
Men	59	51	72	53	22
Women	47	42	81	80	16
January 1966					
Men	54	47	74	57	29
Women	59	41	69	68	24
January 1967					
Men	54	31	88	75	14
Women	59	35	86	78	9

12

GOING ON RECORD

About half of the contents of my original manuscript for *Living With Art* (A. Kroch & Son) was on color. The book was published in 1940 without the information on color.

When the Color Research Institute was established in 1945, I edited the chapters on color; in 1947, *Colors: What They Can Do for You* (Liveright) was published.

During our first few years in business, there was a demand for color guidance. *Colors: What They Can Do for You* went into a second edition in 1948.

I developed a color system with 4,800 colors, derived from the three subtractive primaries (process colors used by printers). This color system containing 4,800 colors on 48 charts, each with 100 colors facing 100 complementary colors, was published in 1949, as the *Cheskin Color System*.

Soon after the color charts were announced, I was urged to write a book on color specifically directed to marketing. *Color for Profit* was published in 1950 (Liveright).

In 1952 came the *Cheskin Color Wheel* (Macmillan). I produced this after two graphics "experts" told me that such a color wheel could not be produced.

When we began to conduct research in the field of home furnishings, we found a demand for a book on color and design for the home. *How to Color-Tune Your Home* was published in May, 1954 (Macmillan).

Originally, I wrote a 32-page booklet on color and design

in the home to be used as a device to get housewives to cooperate in the Color Research Institute marketing tests. When
it became apparent that there was great interest in the subject, that there was really a great demand for guidance in
home furnishing, I expanded the booklet into a full book.

I was told by some of our clients that *Color for Profit* did
not fill all their needs because it did not provide any technical
information on color as applied to packaging and advertising.
I asked executives of Macmillan, publisher of *How to Color-
Tune Your Home,* whether they would be interested in a
book on color for marketing media. The answer was yes.
Within six months I had the manuscript completed, and in
October, 1954, *Color Guide for Marketing Media* was published.

Of course, none of the color books deals only with color.
There is no such thing as abstract color. Color is a part of
form and space. The books deal with practical problems. Imagery, form, design, and pattern are fully discussed. The psychological aspects of form, color, and arrangement are covered.

Then it became apparent that many marketing men were
not aware that we were using color as a control—as a device
for keeping the test on an unconscious level, as a means of
drawing the attention away from the commercial aspect of the
test and also for validating the consumer sample. (We have
the correct answers to the control test.)

It became clear that the books on color were presenting a
false image of our activities. Although it was true that there
was a great desire for color information, our major income
was not derived from color, but from the research of marketing tools—symbols, marketing themes, packages, designs, ads,
billboards.

Early in 1957, Vance Packard's *The Hidden Persuaders*
(David McKay) appeared. In this book, according to some who
read it, I am depicted as a villain. I suddenly became aware
that a motivation researcher was in some circles considered an

evil character. *The Hidden Persuaders* made people conscious of motivation research and aroused some against it.

It was important, I thought, for me to do something that would explain the actual nature of motivation research and its purpose. I decided to declare myself and spell out that motivation research is merely a means for finding out what people really want. Because people cannot or will not always tell us what they like or why they like an object or product, we have to use special techniques for getting the information.

After some deliberation, I decided to publish a collection of my articles on marketing research that had appeared in business magazines. I thought I should also add some articles about my research by other writers.

Since documentation was of primary importance, it was best, I thought, to use the articles in their original form. I was well aware that such a book would not be a piece of original literature.

In order to give unity to the book and to give it a strong, up-to-date beginning, I wrote four new special articles and arranged to have them appear in business publications, with the understanding they would be reprinted in the book. I asked Van Allen Bradley, editorial writer and literary editor of the *Chicago Daily News,* to help me select sixteen articles out of some forty that had appeared since 1947. Twenty articles, including the four new ones, were assembled into manuscript form and Bradley wrote an introduction. *How to Predict What People Will Buy* was published in the early fall of 1957 (Liveright).

There were a number of criticisms of *How to Predict What People Will Buy.* Some thought it was too elementary and sketchy, which of course I knew it was. "You should write a book that goes deeper into motivation research," one of my clients said. Another told me he thought I should tell more about testing techniques. A third person said that I should reveal a little of how ads and packages are tested on an unconscious level. A fourth recommended that I should address management men and point out why they should use marketing research. A fifth suggested that I should tell about my background and how I began testing on an unconscious level.

It became clear to me that there was a need for a comprehensive book on controlled motivation research. I spent evenings and Saturdays writing it. *Why People Buy* was published in 1959 (Liveright).

This book primarily shows how to use motivation research for measuring the effectiveness of packages and ads. It does not cover other areas in which motivation research plays a major role.

Therefore, I again became busy evenings and Saturdays, writing another book. *Basis for Marketing Decision* was published in 1961 (Liveright). In this book, I go deeper into consumer motivation research methodology and I cover aspects that are not covered in the earlier book. Reports of studies of attitudes of employees, of corporate images, of institutions, and of publications are included.

It soon became clear to me that my books were disseminating information and were promoting an understanding of how marketing research is conducted on an unconscious level. This was educating marketing research people, but was not reaching businessmen and marketing and advertising managers.

Therefore, I got busy writing a book for marketers, with emphasis on communication. *Business Without Gambling* was published in 1963 (Quadrangle). This book also contains many reports of studies, mostly of marketing tools. I have been told that it is illuminating and revealing.

In 1964, I had still another book published, *Problem-Directed Men* (Bobbs-Merrill), which deals with socio-economic problems, based on my testimony in Washington before two committees: Senator Philip D. Hart's committee on packaging and Congressman Dante B. Fascell's committee on International Organizations and Movements.

Each of the four business books is filled with case histories, with studies of well-known brands. They document research activities and they validate research results. These books document research projects beginning with 1945. The books and also many of the articles are a record of pioneering work. They deal with marketing successes in which LCA–CRI research played a role.

Several people have asked me why I write so many books. My wife says I write books and articles because I am basically a teacher. However, my conscious reason is to go on record— to document my case histories, to establish my principles, and to record my research results.

Did any other marketing research men conduct experimental studies in motivation research before or at the time I did?

Van Allen Bradley found that I was the first marketing specialist to use the terms "involuntary reactions," "unconscious mind," "brand image," "corporate image," "indirect approach," "unconscious level testing," "motivation research," "sensation transference," "symbolism," "prestige identification," "ego involvement," and "ocular measurements."

Vance Packard, in his research for *The Hidden Persuaders* and *The Waste Makers,* could find no literature on motivation research dated before 1948. The article, "Indirect Approach to Market Reactions," written by me in collaboration with L. B. Ward of the Harvard Business School, appeared in the *Harvard Business Review,* September, 1948.

Ernest Dichter told me that he conducted motivation research before 1945, and I was told that Burleigh Gardner conducted research in motivation as early as 1945. But there is no literature in the early years on their contributions to the field of investigation on consumer attitudes toward marketing tools—symbols, marketing themes, packages, and ads.

Have any marketing or advertising specialists arrived at conclusions like mine?

David Ogilvy was among the first admen to use LCA–CRI research. He understood, I thought, the concept of conducting marketing research on an unconscious level.

Rosser Reeves of Ted Bates (another agency for which I have conducted research) was aware more than a dozen years ago that the only vital role of creativity is to produce the most effective communication, the kind of communication that motivates.

In a letter of June 21, 1965, Rosser Reeves commented on the chapter on communication in my book *Business Without Gambling*. "These are words that should be engraved in brass. It is quite appalling to me that an enormously high percentage of the writers today would deny these statements—and the business is drifting more and more to writers who swing way out, because they find it more fun out there."

In all my marketing books—*Business Without Gambling, Basis for Marketing Decision, Why People Buy,* and *How to Predict What People Will Buy,* and in dozens of articles published in business publications since 1947, I stressed:

1. Consumers consciously buy products, not packages. They are not aware that they are motivated by the package.
2. People do not know that they are motivated by advertising. The best ads, the ads that sell products, draw attention to and inspire an interest in the product, not the advertising.
3. An effective advertising program can be a huge success in selling a high-grade product in an optically correct and psychologically potent package. (Although David Ogilvy does not assign importance to the package in his book, he knows that the package is a vital factor in the success of advertising.)
4. Some ad programs do more harm than good. They alienate consumers.
5. A new package may promote more business or it may lose the old customers and not gain many new ones. A package should be improved, not changed, if the brand has a good share of the market.
6. The marketing theme or headline is the most vital factor in an ad or commercial. If it is weak, the ad is worthless.
7. To be effective, an ad does not have to be recalled consciously. Ads motivate consumers on an unconscious level. The package on the ad has to be recalled so that it is recognized in the store, but it need not be associated with the ad. (Most people will not remember where they have seen the package.)

8. You cannot find out whether an ad or a package is an effective marketing tool by asking people how they like the ad or package, because consumers consciously are not interested in the ad or package; they are interested in the product.
9. Hard sell does not mean great consumer buying. The best kind of selling makes the consumer want to buy without being aware of the selling.
10. In an affluent society like ours, over 90 percent of the products sold are to satisfy psychological wants—styling, status, pleasure-giving commodities, not biological necessities—hamburger or fish, cabbage or onions and bread.

Going on record is vital in every field. In marketing—packaging and advertising—it is most important. Claims are rampant. Validation is established with documentation.

PART III

HOW THEY SUCCEED

1

INTERNATIONAL REGISTER
COMPANY

THE FOLLOWING are reports of studies of two new products. The name test for one of the new products, outdoor lights, and one of the tests of the new Clock-Time • All are reproduced here:

The research showed that both products would have great success, which indeed they have had.

ASSOCIATION TEST: Five Brand Names
for Outdoor Lights

Sample: 400 Home-owners   *July 28, 1965*
family income $10,000 or over

ANALYSIS

Of the five brand names for outdoor lights, Malibu Lights has the greatest consumer acceptance.
Name E also has considerable acceptance.
The other three brand names do not have much acceptance.
Malibu Lights has 72 percent favorable associations and 35 percent preference.
The total number of favorable responses (favorable impact) is very high, 1,280 for Malibu Lights.

Malibu Lights rates higher than any of the other brands with most of the favorable attitude terms.

With "most expensive," Malibu Lights and Name E rate about equally high; with "brightest light" and "best for Christmas lighting," Name E rates higher than Malibu Lights.

In both test areas and among both men and women the pattern of response is similar; Malibu Lights and Name E have greater acceptance than the other three brands.

The test results show clearly that Malibu Lights is the best of the five brand names for outdoor lights. Name E also rates high.

The other three brand names do not rate high enough to be given consideration.

Percentage of Favorable and Unfavorable Associations

	Malibu Lights	Name B	Name C	Name D	Name E
Favorable	72	33	33	43	72
Unfavorable	28	67	67	57	28

Preference

	Number	Percent
Malibu Lights	140	35
Name B	52	13
Name C	46	11
Name D	50	12
Name E	112	28

ASSOCIATION TEST: Five Brand Names
for Outdoor Lights

Number of Associations

Favorable	Malibu Lights	Name B	Name C	Name D	Name E
Highest quality	144	51	35	49	121
Lasts longest	116	59	58	67	99
Lowest operating cost	106	64	62	64	97
Most attractive	138	55	46	50	111
Easiest on the eyes	112	66	61	60	99
Most up-to-date	130	51	54	53	111
Most expensive	111	55	58	63	112
Brightest light	92	60	66	75	106
Best for patio entertaining	104	69	69	68	90
Best for Christmas lighting	94	46	60	72	127
Best gift	133	51	43	61	111
Total	**1,280**	**627**	**612**	**682**	**1,184**

Unfavorable					
Lowest quality	46	120	118	74	42
Does not last longest	36	121	125	78	38
Highest operating cost	37	103	116	93	51
Least attractive	51	114	119	85	30
Hardest on the eyes	51	114	87	83	62
Least up-to-date	63	105	105	64	62
Least expensive	51	123	117	74	35
Least bright	50	126	115	78	31
Not best for patio entertaining	35	107	116	96	45
Not best for Christmas lighting	39	111	135	93	21
Not best gift	49	104	116	83	47
Total	**508**	**1,248**	**1,269**	**901**	**464**
Grand total	**1,788**	**1,875**	**1,881**	**1,583**	**1,648**

ASSOCIATION TEST: Attitudes Toward Clock-Time • All

Sample: 401 Respondents   *July 7, 1965*
income $10,000 or over

ANALYSIS

The Clock-Time • All has considerable consumer acceptance in both test areas. (Half of the respondents saw the actual Clock-Time • All; the other half responded to photos. There was no significant difference in the results.)

NEW YORK:

The Clock-Time • All has 84 percent favorable associations; 88 percent among men and 80 percent among women.

It rates much higher with each of the favorable attitude terms except "desirable for living room" than with the unfavorable attitude terms.

In the choice of one Clock-Time • All or two Time • Alls, the preference is 72 percent for the Clock-Time • All and 28 percent for two Time • Alls. Among men the preference is 60 percent for the Clock-Time • All and among women it is 84 percent.

Among men, the Clock-Time • All is more frequently associated with $29.95 and $34.95 than with the other prices. The majority of women indicate that the price of the Clock-Time • All is $24.95.

CHICAGO:

The Clock-Time • All has 84 percent favorable associations; 85 percent among men and 83 percent among women.

It rates much higher with each of the favorable attitude terms except "desirable for living room" than with the unfavorable attitude terms.

In the choice of one Clock-Time • All or two Time • Alls, among both men and women, the preference is 69 percent for the Clock-Time • All and 31 percent for two Time • Alls.

Among men, the Clock-Time • All has about an equal number of associations with $24.95, $29.95, and $34.95. The majority of women respondents indicate the price is $24.95.

CONCLUSION

The test results show that the Clock-Time • All has substantial consumer acceptance in both New York and Chicago and among both men and women.

Men respondents place a higher value on the Clock-Time • All than do the women respondents. This is shown by the fact that among men, there are more associations with $29.95 and $34.95; among women the majority of price associations are with $24.95.

ASSOCIATION TEST: Attitudes Toward Clock-Time • All

Percentage of Favorable and Unfavorable Associations

Areas	Men	Women	Total
New York			
Favorable	88	80	84
Unfavorable	12	20	16
Chicago			
Favorable	85	83	84
Unfavorable	15	17	16

Percentage of Preference

Areas	Men	Women	Total
New York			
Clock-Time • All (one)	60	84	72
Time • All (two)	40	16	28
Chicago			
Clock-Time • All (one)	69	69	69
Time • All (two)	31	31	31

ASSOCIATION TEST: Attitudes Toward Clock-Time • All

Area: New York

Number of Associations

Favorable	101 Men	101 Women	202 Total
High quality	94	100	194
Useful	94	94	188
Provides protection	94	76	170
Desirable for living room	55	42	97
Suitable for office	94	62	156
Desirable for bedroom	88	79	167
Would consider for gift	94	75	169
Attractive	94	89	183
Modern	94	99	193
Expensive	94	75	169
In good taste	94	95	189
For me	79	78	157
Total	**1,068**	**964**	**2,032**
Unfavorable			
Low quality	7	1	8
Not useful	7	7	14
Does not provide protection	7	25	32
Not desirable for living room	46	59	105
Not suitable for office	7	39	46
Not desirable for bedroom	13	22	35
Would not consider for gift	7	26	33
Not attractive	7	12	19
Not modern	7	2	9
Not expensive	7	26	33
In poor taste	7	6	13
Not for me	22	23	45
Total	**144**	**248**	**392**
Grand total	**1,212**	**1,212**	**2,424**

ASSOCIATION TEST: **Attitudes Toward Clock-Time • All**

Area: Chicago

Number of Associations

Favorable	99 Men	100 Women	199 Total
High quality	93	100	193
Useful	82	94	176
Provides protection	83	83	166
Desirable for living room	50	51	101
Suitable for office	78	71	149
Desirable for bedroom	80	75	155
Would consider for gift	80	81	161
Attractive	97	90	187
Modern	98	100	198
Expensive	92	65	157
In good taste	97	100	197
For me	77	82	159
Total	1,007	992	1,999

Unfavorable			
Low quality	5	—	5
Not useful	17	6	23
Does not provide protection	16	16	32
Not desirable for living room	49	49	98
Not suitable for office	21	29	50
Not desirable for bedroom	17	25	42
Would not consider for gift	19	19	38
Not attractive	2	10	12
Not modern	—	—	—
Not expensive	7	34	41
In poor taste	1	—	1
Not for me	22	18	40
Total	176	206	382
Grand total	1,183	1,198	2,381

2

QUALITY BAKERS OF AMERICA

THE REPORTS reproduced here represent eighteen years of research of packaging and advertising for Quality Bakers of America.

I chose reports for this book that serve as examples of the various kinds of tests that are used for measuring the effectiveness of marketing tools—visibility, readability and eye-movement tests of packages; eye-movement tests of ads; controlled, structured, association tests of brand symbols, packages, marketing themes and ads.

ASSOCIATION TEST: Miss Sunbeam Image
(without identity)

Sample: 200 Housewives   *November 10, 1949*

ANALYSIS

The Miss Sunbeam image is associated with "one product" by 141 housewives (out of 200) and with "several products" by 59.

210

Of the 200 housewives, 196 (98 percent) identified the Miss Sunbeam image with bread.

Of the 200 housewives, 63 (32 percent) identified the Miss Sunbeam image with "Little Miss Sunbeam," 48 (24 percent) with "Miss Sunbeam" or "Sunbeam."

Of the 200 housewives, 174 (87 percent) identified the Miss Sunbeam image (without identity) with Sunbeam.

The Miss Sunbeam image has 91 percent favorable bread associations. It has a large number of associations with all of the favorable attitude words, except with "high price."

Number of Associations

Favorable	
High quality	185
Good	193
High-grade product	192
Full of energy	173
Superior	184
High price	88
Appealing	190
More minerals	188
High nutrition	189
More vitamins	191
Desirable	191
Total	**1,964 (91%)**
Unfavorable	
Low quality	8
Bad	6
Low-grade product	7
Not full of energy	25
Inferior	9
Low price	94
Unappealing	10
Less minerals	9
Low nutrition	7
Less vitamins	6
Undesirable	9
Total	**190 (9%)**

OCULAR MEASUREMENTS: Three Sunbeam Bread Ads

April 30, 1954

ANALYSIS

The eye-movement tests show that the three ads are good. However, they also show that they could be still more effective.

I think the eye-movement test-ratings would be excellent if the cold cuts, toast, soup, and meat loaf illustrations had greater depth and contrast. It is possible that the line drawings do not have enough contrast to compete with the halftones.

Perhaps a heavier frame around each appetite-appeal illustration would cause the eyes to turn to each of the appetite-appeal images. Maybe each illustration should be framed separately, instead of using a dividing line between illustrations.

Also, *you* and *extra-something* at the top should be given still greater emphasis so that the consumer is forced to read the copy at first glance.

Ad #62A   **Rating**

   Eye Movement—Eyes fell on Miss Sunbeam where attention   B (Good)
      was held, dropped to loaf of bread where at-
      tention was held, then to *3 Great Food Extras*
      and left the page.

Ad #62NA

   Eye Movement—Eyes fell on boy eating bread where atten-   B (Good)
      tion was held, dropped to loaf of bread
      where attention was held, then to *3 Great
      Food Extras* and left the page.

Ad #8

   Eye Movement—Eyes fell on Miss Sunbeam where attention   B (Good)
      was held, dropped to loaf of bread where at-
      tention was held, then to *it's Energy packed*
      and left the page.

ASSOCIATION TEST: QBA Ad Theme—
"Look Ma—No Holes!"

Sample: 200 Housewives   *August 13, 1959*

ANALYSIS

The QBA ad theme "Look Ma—No Holes!" has 76 percent favorable associations.

The theme is associated with an old product (rather than a new product) by 108 out of 200 housewives.

Of the 200 housewives, 197 associate the theme with bread and 189 associate it with Sunbeam.

This test shows clearly that this commercial has reached 98 percent of the consumers, which is tremendous saturation.

**Percentage of Favorable and
Unfavorable Associations**

Favorable	76
Unfavorable	24

ASSOCIATION TEST: QBA Ad Theme— "Look Ma—No Holes!"

Number of Associations

Favorable	
Good	166
High quality	169
Superior product	164
Costly ingredients	163
Better than other brands	106
Good to eat	174
Beneficial	171
Friendly	174
Interesting	120
Not irritating	136
Little girl	131
Total	**1,674**

Unfavorable	
Bad	34
Low quality	30
Inferior product	34
Cheap ingredients	37
Same as other brands	94
Not good to eat	26
Not beneficial	28
Unfriendly	26
Boring	79
Irritating	64
Little boy	69
Total	**521**

Unclassified	
New product	91
Old product	108
Grand total	**2,394**

ASSOCIATION TEST: Miss Sunbeam Image
(without identity)

Sample: 1,400 Housewives   *September 19, 1960*

ANALYSIS

There are 95 percent favorable associations with the Miss Sunbeam Image (without identity), 98 percent in both Houston and Sacramento, 96 percent in both Philadelphia and Atlanta, and 88 percent in New York.

The Miss Sunbeam Image rates high with all the favorable associations. It has a large number of associations with "familiar" and "real little girl."

Number of Favorable and Unfavorable Associations

	200 Houston	400 Phil.	201 New York	204 Sac.	395 Atlanta	1,400 Total
Favorable	1,964	3,834	1,754	2,000	3,798	13,350
Unfavorable	35	165	248	37	147	632
Total	1,999	3,999	2,002	2,037	3,945	13,982

Percentage of Favorable and Unfavorable Associations

	200 Houston	400 Phil.	201 New York	204 Sac.	395 Atlanta	1,400 Total
Favorable	98	96	88	98	96	95
Unfavorable	2	4	12	2	4	5

ASSOCIATION TEST: Miss Sunbeam Image
(without identity)

Number of Associations

Favorable	200 Houston	400 Phil.	201 New York	204 Sac.	395 Atlanta	1,400 Total
Wholesome	196	379	188	201	390	1,354
Attractive	197	382	178	198	368	1,323
Happy	199	383	181	201	394	1,358
Healthy	196	386	183	203	393	1,361
Loved	198	387	180	203	390	1,358
Alert	192	384	164	200	355	1,295
Full of energy	195	385	168	198	384	1,330
Appealing	196	382	170	196	367	1,311
Intelligent	197	386	172	201	384	1,340
I like her	198	380	170	199	373	1,320
Total	**1,964**	**3,834**	**1,754**	**2,000**	**3,798**	**13,350**
Unfavorable						
Not wholesome	3	21	12	3	3	42
Unattractive	3	18	23	6	26	76
Unhappy	1	16	18	2	1	38
Not healthy	4	14	16	1	2	37
Neglected	2	13	20	1	5	41
Not alert	8	16	37	4	40	105
Not full of energy	5	15	31	6	10	67
Unappealing	4	18	31	8	27	88
Stupid	3	14	29	1	11	58
I don't like her	2	20	31	5	22	80
Total	**35**	**165**	**248**	**37**	**147**	**632**
Unclassified						
Familiar	197	320	108	188	373	1,186
Unfamiliar	3	80	92	16	22	213
Real little girl	185	318	81	127	294	1,005
Imaginary little girl	15	82	120	77	101	395
Grand total	**2,399**	**4,799**	**2,403**	**2,445**	**4,735**	**16,781**

H. C. Price Tower
Oklahoma

Johnson Wax Building
Wisconsin

CADILLAC

LINCOLN CONTINENTAL

The 1961 Lincoln Continental and competitive car with architectural controls used in testing the styling of the Continental. The building at the right and the Lincoln Continental rated much higher than the building at the left and the competitive car.

The Standard symbol, oval in red, white, and blue, with torch, was adopted in 1945, on the basis of extensive marketing research. It is still the most effective symbol in the oil industry.

Five proposed signs that were tested in 1945 for Standard Oil of Indiana, now the American Oil Company.

The Dove package symbolizes the high quality of the product. It rated high in display effectiveness (visibility, readability, and eye movement) and in favorable connotations (controlled association test).

At the left, Imperial margarine in the original package, introduced in 1955; at the right, the new package introduced in 1965.

Package changes that coincided with the market growth of Good Luck margarine. From the left, the first package; second, package that was introduced in 1952; third, package introduced about two years later; fourth, package that was introduced in 1960 and is essentially the same now. Each change was made on the basis of thorough research.

At the left, one of the old Betty Crocker packages. In the center, the package introduced in 1953. At the right, the package introduced about a year later. Each change resulted in a great increase in sales.

At the left, the original Crisco label; in the middle, the label introduced in 1947, on the basis of research; at the right, the label introduced about two years later on the basis of further package development and research. To date, the label has remained basically the same.

New Salada tea package, at the left, rated much more than twice as high in favorable associations than the old package at the right.

At the left, old Hires labels and carton; at the right, new package. The association test and the ocular measurements showed that the new package will bring a great increase in sales.

At the left, the original brown Philip Morris package; in the center, the package introduced in 1953; at the right, the present plastic package. Each change was made on the basis of extensive research.

At the left, Benson & Hedges in the old Parliament package. (Smokers of the original Parliament became smokers of Benson & Hedges; sales were about the same.) At the right, the new Benson & Hedges package. The research showed that the new package endowed Benson & Hedges with even more status.

At the left, the original Parliament package. At the right, the package introduced in 1954, launching Parliament as a popular brand.

Two experimental Marlboro packages. The one at the left was the designer's "logical" package; it shows the type of cigarette the package contains. The one at the right has the Philip Morris crest; the research showed that the package with the crest rated much higher in quality connotations.

At the left, the original Marlboro package. At right, the package introduced in 1953, which was the beginning of Marlboro becoming a major brand.

A Philip Morris ad that rated high in eye flow (eye-movement test) and in favorable associations (controlled association test).

A Parliament ad that rated high in eye flow (eye-movement test) and in favorable associations (controlled association test).

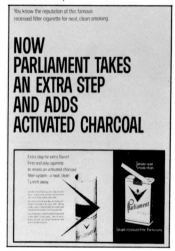

A Marlboro ad that rated high in eye flow (eye-movement test) and in favorable associations (controlled association test).

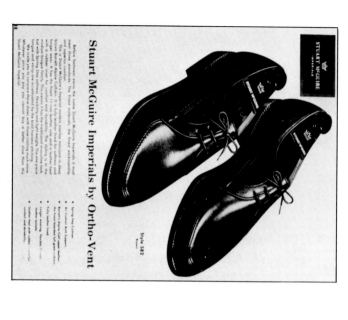

A page from Stuart McGuire shoe catalog that rated high in eye flow and attention-holding (eye-movement test).

A page from Eaton's catalog (Canada) that rated high in eye flow and attention-holding (eye-movement test).

1	**Nescafé**
2	**NESCAFÉ**
3	**NESCAFÉ**
4	**NESCAFÉ**

No. 1 is the proposed "modern" logo. No. 2 is the old logo. No. 3 is a proposed modification of the old logo. No. 4 is another proposed modification of the old logo. The No. 3 logo rated highest in readability and in favorable associations.

At the left, old Nescafé jar; at the right, new jar. The research (controlled association test) showed that the new, narrower jar, with the new, higher cap with crown symbol and the new (No. 3) logo motivated many new consumers to buy Nescafé.

At left, Miss Sunbeam trademark, Quality Bakers of America. It rated over 90 percent in favorable associations in 1949 and now rates over 95 percent. It is one of the most effective marketing symbols.

At the right, a Sunbeam ad that rated very high in eye flow (eye-movement test) and in favorable associations (controlled association test).

Below, two proposed Sunbeam bread wrappers. The wrapper at the left rated much higher in display effectiveness (ocular measurements) and in psychological connotations (controlled association test).

BREAD WITH A BONUS!

At the left, the original Blue Star Potato Chips package; at the right, the first change based on research. It brought an immediate increase in sales.

The present Blue Star carton is still more effective as a marketing tool. It rated very high in display effectiveness (ocular measurements) and in favorable associations (controlled association test).

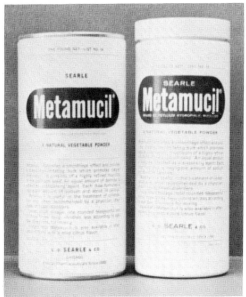

At the left, the original G. D. Searle Metamucil package; at the right, the new package in which the product rated much higher in favorable associations. The research showed that the new package will result in increased sales.

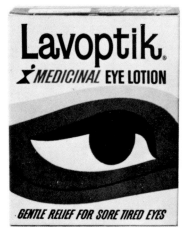
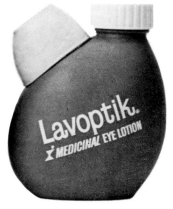

Lavoptik eye lotion bottle and carton that rated very high in favorable associations and in high quality connotations. The carton also rated high in display effectiveness (ocular measurements).

Consoweld ad that rated high in eye flow and attention holding (eye-movement test) and in the field test (association test).

Clock-Time·All produced by International Register Company rated 84 percent in favorable associations in the LCA association test conducted in 1965.

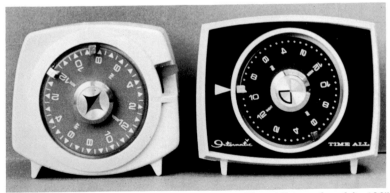

At the left, old Time·All; at the right, new Time·All introduced in 1965 which became a great success, as predicted by marketing research.

Shadow Ban light bulb package, designed to express high quality.

Light bulb display of the new packages of General Electric of Canada. The new packages, developed with the aid of research, became the basis for a marketing program resulting in a great sales increase.

OCULAR MEASUREMENTS: Two Sunbeam
Bread Band Designs

December 18, 1964

ANALYSIS

SUNBEAM BAND FOR WHITE BREAD—DESIGN NO. 1

The visibility of the band as a whole is very good.

Readability of *White* is very good.

Eye flow and attention-holding are only fair because there is considerable hesitation and only *White* holds attention.

SUNBEAM BAND FOR WHITE BREAD—DESIGN NO. 2

The visibility of the band as a whole is excellent.

Readability of *White* is excellent.

Eye flow and attention-holding are excellent.

The ocular measurements show clearly that from a display aspect, Design No. 1 has a great weakness and Design No. 2 is excellent.

Design No. 1	
Ocular measurements	**Rating**
Visibility	87
Readability—White	84
Eye Movement—After considerable hesitation, eyes fell on Miss Sunbeam, moved to *Sunbeam*, to *White* and left package. Attention was held on *White* only.	C (Fair)
Design No. 2	
Ocular measurements	**Rating**
Visibility	92
Readability—White	90
Eye Movement—Eyes fell on *White*, moved to Miss Sunbeam, to *Sunbeam* and left package. Attention was held at each point.	A (Excellent)

ASSOCIATION TEST: Two Stroehmann Sunbeam Pride Winner Bread Wrappers—Present vs. Proposed

Sample: 400 Mothers   *March 23, 1965*

ANALYSIS

The Proposed Bread Wrapper has greater consumer acceptance than the Present Bread Wrapper.

In Williamsport (Stroehmann Area) the Proposed Wrapper rates a little higher than the Present Wrapper in favorable associations and in preference.

In Rochester (Non-Stroehmann Area) the Proposed Wrapper rates much higher than the Present Wrapper in favorable associations and in preference.

WILLIAMSPORT, PA. (STROEHMANN AREA):

The bread in the Proposed Wrapper has 52 percent favorable associations; the bread in the Present Wrapper has 48 percent favorable associations.

The preference is 54 percent for the bread in the Proposed Wrapper and 46 percent for the bread in the Present Wrapper.

Each bread has about the same number of associations with most of the favorable attitude terms. However, the bread in the Proposed Wrapper rates considerably higher with "stays fresh longer."

The bread in the Proposed Wrapper also rates somewhat higher with "higher calories" and much higher with "more expensive."

ROCHESTER, N. Y. (NON-STROEHMANN AREA):

The bread in the Proposed Wrapper has 63 percent favorable associations; the bread in the Present Wrapper has 37 percent favorable associations.

The preference is 65 percent for the bread in the Proposed Wrapper and 35 percent for the bread in the Present Wrapper.

The bread in the Proposed Wrapper has a larger number of associations with each of the favorable attitude terms than does the bread in the Present Wrapper. It rates particularly high with "more nourishing." The bread in the Proposed Wrapper also rates higher with "higher calories" and "more expensive."

CONCLUSION

The test results show clearly that the Proposed Wrapper is more effective than the Present Wrapper.

3

GENERAL ELECTRIC OF CANADA

THE FOLLOWING was reported by an executive of Canadian General Electric:

"Packaging programs have played a major role in the success of our retail products, especially over the past five years. As a matter of fact, we have gained an excellent reputation in the industry for exploiting the sales opportunities involved in integrating packaging to give strong support to our total market approach.

"For example, in 1961 we developed a new merchandising approach for white-coated and inside-frosted household light bulbs. The approach was designed to present our product to consumers at the point of purchase in terms and values meaningful to them.

"This situation called for a completely new packaging program, since packaging had to do most of the job.

"Before the new program, white bulbs (the higher quality, premium-priced product) represented 2 out of 10 sales for G.E. Since the introduction of the new packaging based on a truly consumer-oriented approach, white-bulb sales (now branded Shadow Ban bulbs) have grown faster than any other product and now represent 6 out of 10 sales.

"Shadow Ban has become synonymous with outstanding bulb merchandising in Canadian retailing, and is the outstanding product success story in the lamp industry. Despite little media support, Shadow Ban is the best-known light bulb brand to Canadian consumers. The role of the packaging program in achieving these results has been an overwhelming success.

"Another top success story is our Christmas lights product line. Again in 1961 we developed an entirely new marketing program to generate a strong consumer pull. A comprehensive packaging program was developed, involving new product names, terminology, graphics, and shipping cases. While media and other merchandising tools were probably more important to the product line's success, the packaging was a great vehicle for projecting the revitalized G.E. Christmas story not only to the consumer, but to the distributors and retailers as well.

"Sales on this product line leaped from below 4,000,000 units in 1960 to over 20,000,000 units in 1965."

Following are some examples of research that was used for predetermining the marketing effectiveness of the G.E. packages designed under the supervision of Jack Roberts.

ASSOCIATION TEST: General Electric Shadow Ban vs. Two Competitors

Sample: 200 Respondents   *June 29, 1960*

ANALYSIS

The results of this test clearly show that General Electric Shadow Ban with 70 percent total favorable associations is superior to Competition B (48 percent) and Competition A (38 percent).

General Electric Shadow Ban has the greatest number of responses to all favorable associations except for "soft." In association with "soft"

General Electric Shadow Ban is 64, Competition A is 76, Competition B is 58.

With the unclassified associations, General Electric Shadow Ban is considered "expensive" by 85 respondents and "inexpensive" by 56, whereas Competition B has 61 responses to "expensive" and 71 to "inexpensive," and Competition A has 59 responses to "expensive" and 68 to "inexpensive."

General Electric Shadow Ban is considered more "modern" (77) than "old-fashioned" (59).

In the preference part of the test, 50 percent of the respondents indicated a preference for General Electric Shadow Ban, 32 percent for Competition B and 18 percent for Competition A.

This test shows that, without a doubt, the General Electric Shadow Ban package is an effective marketing tool.

Percentage of Favorable and Unfavorable Associations

	General Electric Shadow Ban	Competition A	Competition B
Favorable	70	38	48
Unfavorable	30	62	52

Percentage of Preference

	Men	Women	Total
General Electric Shadow Ban	50	51	50
Competition A	17	19	18
Competition B	33	30	32

ASSOCIATION TEST: General Electric Shadow Ban vs. Two Competitors

Number of Associations

Favorable	General Electric Shadow Ban	Competition A	Competition B
High quality	115	40	46
Good value	91	57	64
Strong light	91	47	63
Even light	110	36	52
Soft	64	76	58
Little eyestrain	90	57	63
Good for reading	100	46	64
Good for work areas	100	45	62
Long-lasting	98	48	65
Superior	100	42	61
Economical	90	53	61
For me	103	50	57
Total	**1,152**	**597**	**716**

Unfavorable			
Low quality	33	87	64
Poor value	40	77	65
Weak light	41	85	64
Uneven light	36	88	61
Harsh	52	71	78
Much eyestrain	47	72	66
Poor for reading	40	91	50
Poor for work areas	35	85	54
Not long-lasting	41	81	65
Inferior	32	93	61
Wasteful	48	72	64
Not for me	38	87	71
Total	**483**	**989**	**763**

Unclassified			
Expensive	85	59	61
Inexpensive	56	68	71
Modern	77	56	85
Old-fashioned	59	68	57
Grand total	**1,912**	**1,837**	**1,753**

OCULAR MEASUREMENTS: General Electric
Shadow Ban Revised Ad Layouts

August 31, 1960

Layout 1:3   **Rating**

Eye Movement—Eyes fell on partial blue panel at top of   A (Excellent)
    page, moved to *now*, to *light bulbs that*
    don't glare at you!, to bulb on blue
    panel, to *Shadow, GE, Ban;* to *100,*
    dropped to yellow panel at bottom left,
    moved to Mr. Magoo, to *GE* and left ad.

Layout 2:3

Eye Movement—Eyes fell on *now*, moved to *light bulbs*   A (Excellent)
    that don't glare at you!, to bulb on blue
    panel, to *Shadow, GE, Ban;* to *100,*
    dropped to yellow panel at bottom left,
    moved to Mr. Magoo, to *GE* and left ad.

Layout 3:3

Eye Movement—After some hesitation, eyes fell on bulb   B (Good)
    on blue panel, moved to *Shadow, GE,*
    Ban; to *100,* dropped to yellow panel at
    bottom left, moved to Mr. Magoo, to *GE*
    and left ad.

ASSOCIATION TEST: General Electric Christmas Bulb
Package vs. Three Competitive Packages

Sample: 600 Respondents   *April 28, 1961*

ANALYSIS

In the preference part of the test, 44 percent prefer General Electric, 26 percent prefer Competition A, 9 percent prefer Competition B, and 21 percent prefer Competition C.

General Electric has the greatest preference by both women and men and in all three areas.

General Electric has 87 percent favorable associations, Competition A has 48 percent, Competition B has 24 percent, and Competition C has 36 percent.

The percentage of favorable associations with General Electric are 83 percent among women and 91 percent among men.

In the three areas, the percentage of favorable associations with General Electric are 87 percent in Toronto, 81 percent in Vancouver, and 93 percent in French Montreal.

General Electric has the largest number of associations with each of the favorable attitude words and phrases.

"Made in Canada" is associated with General Electric by 90 percent, with Competition A by 89 percent, with Competition B by 28 percent and with Competition C by 59 percent.

The average of the price associations is 53 cents with both General Electric and Competition A, 48 cents with Competition B, and 50 cents with Competition C.

Of the 600 respondents 58 percent prefer an "assembled unit of cord and bulbs" and 42 percent prefer a "cord unit in which you put bulbs of your own selection." However, in Toronto the choice is 50-50.

Percentage of Favorable and Unfavorable Associations

	General Electric	Competition A	Competition B	Competition C
Favorable	87	48	24	36
Unfavorable	13	52	76	64

ASSOCIATION TEST: General Electric Christmas Bulb Package vs. Three Competitive Packages

Number of Associations

Favorable	General Electric	Competition A	Competition B	Competition C
Highest quality	289	139	51	121
Most safe	277	151	56	116
Most reliable	297	147	42	111
Best buy	280	141	48	131
Longest life	277	152	52	118
Most attractive	309	120	80	89
Most modern	293	124	95	87
Superior	301	146	52	99
Brightest	328	108	112	51
Most appealing	277	124	94	103
Distinctive	287	115	95	100
Most festive	297	120	95	84
Total	**3,512**	**1,587**	**872**	**1,210**
Unfavorable				
Lowest quality	53	126	250	171
Least safe	40	112	301	145
Least reliable	47	87	305	161
Poorest buy	45	99	285	171
Shortest life	48	86	298	168
Least attractive	43	179	190	185
Least modern	41	170	197	192
Inferior	44	101	276	179
Dullest	29	230	138	202
Least appealing	41	163	206	189
Ordinary	62	176	171	191
Least festive	38	189	170	199
Total	**531**	**1,718**	**2,787**	**2,153**
Grand total	**4,043**	**3,305**	**3,659**	**3,363**

4

LEVER BROTHERS

LCA–CRI research for Lever Brothers has been covered in another part of the book. The reports, in part reproduced here, are representative of the kind of research we have been conducting for Lever since 1952.

The first package designs for the Dove bar and Imperial margarine were put through all of the necessary tests. Both Dove and Imperial were launched with effective packages. The tests reproduced here show that after several years, new packages were developed that were more effective marketing tools than the original designs.

ASSOCIATION TEST: Present White Dove Wrapper vs. Proposed Wrapper Design

Sample: 400 Housewives   *April 22, 1963*

ANALYSIS

The results of this test show clearly that the Proposed Wrapper Design has greater consumer acceptance than the Present White Dove Wrapper. Dove in the Proposed Wrapper Design has a higher percentage of favorable associations and preference than Dove in the Present Wrapper, in each of the classifications of the consumer sample.

Dove in the Proposed Wrapper Design has a larger number of associations than Dove in the Present Wrapper with each of the favorable attitude terms.

The results of the ocular measurements and stacking test show that the Proposed Wrapper Design has display effectiveness. The field test shows that it is also effective psychologically. Therefore, the Proposed Wrapper Design for White Dove is a highly potent marketing tool.

**Percentage of Favorable and
Unfavorable Associations**

Categories	Present Wrapper		Proposed Wrapper	
	Favorable	Un-favorable	Favorable	Un-favorable
Total	38	62	62	38
Area				
East	38	62	62	38
Midwest	37	63	63	37
Age				
Under 35 years	37	63	63	37
Over 35 years	38	62	62	38
Income				
$5,000 to $7,500	39	61	61	39
$7,500 to $10,000	36	64	64	36
Users				
Dove	41	59	59	41
Non-Dove	37	63	63	37

OCULAR MEASUREMENTS: Proposed Dove Wrapper Design

April 22, 1963

ANALYSIS

Visibility of the package as a whole is very good.

Readability of Dove is fairly good. Considering that this is a beauty product, it is as good as it should be.

However, eye flow and attention-holding are good, but not excellent, because there is an element of hesitation. (I believe the hesitation is caused by the conflict of the white space with the logo.)

In a stack, the eye flow over the package is smooth and attention is held. No hesitation was evident in the stacking test.

Ocular Measurements	Rating
Visibility	84
Readability—Dove	76
Eye Movement—Eyes fell on gold dove and, after some hesitation, dropped to Dove and left package. Attention was held at both points.	B (Good)
Stacking Test— (six on six) Eyes fell on package at upper left, moved to second package, to third package, to fourth, fifth, and sixth packages and left stack. Attention was held on each package.	A (Excellent)

ASSOCIATION TEST: Two Imperial Packages— Present Gold vs. Proposed Gold

Sample: 400 Housewives   *July 8, 1965*

ANALYSIS

The Proposed Gold Imperial Package has greater consumer acceptance than the Present Gold Package.

The margarine in the Proposed Package has 69 percent favorable associations, that in the Present Package 31 percent.

The preference is 69 percent for the margarine in the Proposed Package and 31 percent for the margarine in the Present Package.

The margarine in the Proposed Package rates much higher with each of the favorable attitude terms than does that in the Present Package.

The margarine in the Proposed Package is also much more frequently considered "higher-priced" than is the margarine in the Present Package.

Among respondents in each area and in each age and income category, the Proposed Package rates much higher than the Present Package. The Proposed Package also rates much higher than the Present Package among both Imperial users and non-Imperial users.

The test results show clearly that the Proposed Gold Imperial Package is superior to the Present Gold Imperial Package.

ASSOCIATION TEST: Two Imperial Packages—
Present Gold vs. Proposed Gold

SUMMARY TABLE

Housewives—Total	Present Gold	Proposed Gold
Favorable associations	31%	69%
Preference	31%	69%
East		
Favorable associations	32%	68%
Preference	34%	66%
Midwest		
Favorable associations	29%	71%
Preference	28%	72%
Under 35 years		
Favorable associations	32%	68%
Preference	32%	68%
35 years or over		
Favorable associations	29%	71%
Preference	30%	70%
Income $5,000 to $7,500		
Favorable associations	31%	69%
Preference	32%	68%
Income $7,500 to $10,000		
Favorable associations	30%	70%
Preference	30%	70%
Imperial users		
Favorable associations	34%	66%
Preference	36%	64%
Non-Imperial users		
Favorable associations	29%	71%
Preference	28%	72%

5

LINCOLN–MERCURY DIVISION
FORD MOTOR COMPANY

THE AUTOMOTIVE INDUSTRY, a basic and vital factor in our economy, has been dominated by two fallacies: 1) that any change in styling annually will promote sales and 2) that anything can be sold if the advertising budget is big.

When I learned that the Ford Motor Company set out to produce a luxury car on the basis of all four pillars—guarantee of performance, styling appeal, right price and "effective" communication, I could see a success story in the automotive industry. Specifically, I was impressed with the newly set policy of having each car individually tested, of driver-testing each car before delivery to the dealer, of giving a full guarantee—labor as well as parts—of testing the styling and the advertising with luxury car buyers and pricing the car to meet the price of competitive cars.

LCA–CRI tests showed clearly that the 1961 Lincoln Continental would become the status car.

The final test of the 1961 Lincoln Continental is reproduced at the end of this chapter.

from THE CONTINENTAL MAGAZINE

January–February, 1962

Louis Cheskin, pioneer in probing public attitudes, explains why the Lincoln Continental is the car with

THE LOOK OF SUCCESS

Interview by C. H. Dykeman

Can people really tell you what they want in styling—in the design of the car they intend to buy?

230

Few pre-marketing research studies have so clearly predicted an outstanding success of a car within weeks of its introduction, as did an association test of the 1961 Lincoln Continental vs. competition.

The editors of *The Continental Magazine* interviewed Louis Cheskin, director of Color Research Institute, president of Louis Cheskin Associates (marketing research), and author of *Basis for Marketing Decision*, in which the study of the Lincoln Continental is included. The prediction of the sweeping popularity of the Lincoln Continental was made on the basis of this study.

Q. Mr. Cheskin, where and how did you conduct your study of attitudes toward the Lincoln Continental?

A. We conducted studies in New York City and Chicago with 4,792 car-owners of over $15,000 income. The major part of this study consisted of controlled association tests.

Q. How could you be so sure that the Continental would be such a great success even before there was a sales trend?

A. We had no difficulty doing this. We tested every new car which was announced as embodying a "new concept." We found that the new Lincoln Continental styling had very great appeal. In fact the Continental topped all cars by a remarkably high rating in favorable associations (88 percent). Only the 1957 Thunderbird came anywhere near with 84 percent. No other car ever had rated over 60 percent in favorable associations before this time.

Q. What do you think most people mean by "styling" in a car?

A. Our sense of sight is the most important of all senses. Styling for most people symbolizes the function of a car. Women especially were attracted by the new lines of the Lincoln Continental. Men called it "classic," "reliable," "lasting," and "desirable."

Q. Were you able to determine what point about the Lincoln Continental besides the styling was particularly well-liked?

A. The fact that the company executives had such confidence in the new Lincoln Continental that they were willing to give a two-year warranty made a deep impression. Of the luxury car owners interviewed, 81 percent associated this with "trouble-free." Also, the price was right, being competitive with other luxury cars which did not rate nearly as high in styling, in mechanical aspects, or in advertising appeal.

Q. Did you ever feel that you had gone out on a limb in predicting the success of the Lincoln Continental?

A. Not for one minute. Like anything else, research can be good or bad. If you base a prediction on the assumption that people can tell you why they make choices, you get misleading answers. If you ask people to be judges, they will give you misleading information. Too small samples of consumers can also mislead. Controlled research conducted on an unconscious level with large enough samples of respondents has on the other hand successfully predicted marketing success or failure for over fifteen years.

Q. What is the most important factor, in your opinion, that has led to Lincoln Continental success?

A. I began to have confidence in the car when I learned that the manufacturer considered the product itself—the performance of the car —most important. I had a report that the Lincoln Continental had the longest road check in American car production history.

Q. You obviously rate product quality high, then, in influencing sales?

A. Yes, I consider quality as the basis for a marketing program. But we must remember that the performance of a car as a means of transportation is only one aspect of its success. The design, the psychological or aesthetic aspect of quality is another. Next comes the character of the advertising, which is communication about the performance and psychological quality. Last is price, which should of course be competitive. All four aspects are important factors in marketing.

Q. One final question. Did the people being interviewed know you were making a test of the Lincoln Continental?

A. We conduct attitude studies. Tests are conducted so that the respondents do not feel we are interested in any one particular product. We want their feelings expressed without their defense mechanisms aroused to influence their responses. We want a reaction from each individual that represents his true feelings. The Lincoln Continental was tested together with other things of interest to the respondent, among which were architectural designs, which are also of general interest.

"Among the top echelon of Cadillac, Imperial, Lincoln buyers, those who shopped for cars priced $5,500 or more, 56.2 percent bought Lincoln Continentals.

"Accordingly, in the first year of marketing its revolutionary concept of prestige automobiles, Lincoln captured No. 1 spot in its own immediate price class."—*Ward's Automotive Reports,* November 6, 1961.

ASSOCIATION TEST: Attitudes Toward Two Luxury
Cars—Lincoln Continental vs. Competitive Car

CONTROL TEST: H. C. Price Tower vs.
Johnson Wax Building (statistics shown in part)

June 29, 1961

ASSOCIATION TEST ANALYSIS

This study shows clearly that in styling the Lincoln Continental is by far superior to the competitive car. However, the Lincoln Continental still does not have a quality image as high as the competitive car.

With *designers,* Lincoln Continental rates overwhelmingly higher than the competitive car with the following associations: greater dignity, in better taste, classical styling, more distinctive, more luxurious, higher quality, greater precision, easier to handle.

With *architects,* Lincoln Continental rates much higher than the competitive car with: greater dignity, in better taste, classical styling, more distinctive, more luxurious.

With *executives,* Lincoln Continental rates considerably higher than the competitive car with: classical styling, greater dignity, in better taste, more distinctive, more luxurious.

With all three groups, the competitive car is associated primarily with more ostentatious and more flamboyant.

Impact is seen in the total number of responses. (Low impact or lack of response indicates indifference or disinterest on the part of the respondents.) The total response or impact is 82 percent among the designers, 67 percent among the architects, and 75 percent among the executives, which shows the different degree of interest in the two cars among the three groups of respondents.

The percentage of favorable associations with each term do not add to 100 percent because all respondents do not react to all the associations.

CONTROL TEST ANALYSIS

The results of the control test show that the design relationship between the two luxury cars and the two architectural examples is apparent to a large majority of the respondents.

The Johnson Wax Building is considered: in better taste, better design, better construction, more practical, more functional. The H. C. Price Tower is considered outdated by a majority of the designers and architects.

A majority of the executives considers the Johnson Wax Building: in better taste, better design, more practical, more functional, and the H. C. Price Tower outdated and better construction.

ASSOCIATION TEST: Attitudes of Designers
toward Two Luxury Cars

Sample: 178 Designers

Percentage of Associations

	Competitive Car	Lincoln Continental
More ostentatious	85	9
Greater dignity	4	92
Classical styling	3	88
More luxurious	19	69
In better taste	4	91
More distinctive	6	87
Higher quality	24	65
Greater precision	23	46
Easier to handle	17	44
More reliable	38	27
Better craftsmanship	34	38
More efficient performance	31	30
More flamboyant	90	5

ASSOCIATION TEST: Attitudes of Architects
toward Two Luxury Cars

Sample: 258 Architects

Percentage of Associations

	Competitive Car	Lincoln Continental
More ostentatious	80	10
Greater dignity	8	82
Classical styling	7	73
More luxurious	23	49
In better taste	8	80
More distinctive	14	71
Higher quality	28	32
Greater precision	23	24
Easier to handle	19	21
More reliable	30	17
Better craftsmanship	24	27
More efficient performance	25	15
More flamboyant	73	10

ASSOCIATION TEST: Attitudes of Executives toward Two Luxury Cars

Sample: 269 Executives

Percentage of Associations

	Competitive Car	Lincoln Continental
More ostentatious	68	17
Greater dignity	20	66
Classical styling	14	70
More luxurious	32	47
In better taste	20	65
More distinctive	22	65
Higher quality	41	36
Greater precision	37	28
Easier to handle	31	25
More reliable	43	19
Better craftsmanship	42	27
More efficient performance	41	19
More flamboyant	61	17

6

PHILIP MORRIS

PHILIP MORRIS is already covered in another part of the book. I have chosen to reproduce here parts of the most interesting studies on the Marlboro and Parliament packages, examples of ocular measurements of Marlboro and Parliament ads and ocular measurements of an Alpine package.

ASSOCIATION TEST: Marlboro Package—
Recessed Tip Cigarette Image vs. Crest Symbol

Sample: 400 Cigarette Smokers   *December 23, 1954*

ANALYSIS

This test with 400 smokers shows that the package with the Crest Symbol has much greater appeal and greater impact than the package with the Recessed Tip Cigarette Image.

Associations listed in order of rank for each package show that 334 out of 400 smokers associate the package with the Recessed Tip Cigarette Image with *inferior,* whereas 345 out of the 400 smokers associate the package with the Crest Symbol with *high quality.*

The relative impact is revealed in that the package with the Recessed Tip Cigarette Image received only 2,395 tallies. The package with the Crest Symbol received 3,734 tallies.

Associations Listed in Order of
Rank for Each Package

Ranks	Recessed Tip Cigarette Image		Crest Symbol	
1	Inferior	334	High quality	345
2	Not for me	306	More attractive	337
3	Ordinary	298	Superior	335
4	Modern	269	More appealing	327
5	Confusing	244	More pleasing	319
6	Feminine	201	Higher price	318
7	Masculine	186	Pride	313
8	Distinctive	74	Distinctive	312
9	More pleasing	73	For me	310
10	Higher price	67	Masculine	212
11	More appealing	66	Feminine	190
12	More attractive	63	Modern	118
13	For me	63	Confusing	104
14	Pride	55	Ordinary	84
15	High quality	49	Not for me	65
16	Superior	47	Inferior	45
Totals		2,395		3,734

OCULAR MEASUREMENTS: Two Marlboro Ads

December 5, 1961

ANALYSIS

The following ocular measurements show that one of the ads is weak and one of them is excellent.

Optically, Ad 1:2 is a very effective ad.

The red *Marlboro* in Ad 2:2 at upper left and the red package are fighting for attention.

Ad 1:2	**Rating**
Eye movement—Eyes fell on cigarette package, moved to man's ear, across mouth and nose, to Marlboro, to the filter cigarette with the unfiltered taste, to cigarette in man's hand and left ad.	A (Excellent)
Ad 2:2	
Eye movement—After some hesitation eyes fell on Marlboro at left, then dropped to man's feet, moved up to head, dropped to Marlboro package at right and left ad.	C (Fair)

ASSOCIATION TEST: (Parliament) Chevron-Crest Symbol

Sample: 600 Cigarette Smokers   *November 14, 1955*

ANALYSIS

This test is quite clear as far as favorable and unfavorable associations are concerned.

I have not seen a test before that had less than 10 percent unfavorable associations. However, there is a question in the associations of *masculine* and *feminine*.

The test now in the field, which is identified as a cigarette package, will show to what extent the masculine association will be brought down and the feminine up by the relationship of the Chevron-Crest Symbol with cigarettes.

Attitude Words Ranked According to
Number of Associations

Ranks	Chevron-Crest Symbol	
1	Attractive	581
2	Good	579
3	Country club	570
4	In good taste	567
5	High quality	564
6	Expensive	563
7	Distinguished	552
8	Mink	542
9	Cadillac	534
10	Formal	533
11	Lends prestige	528
12	Hard-top convertible	517
13	For me	508
14	Masculine	436
15	Feminine	151
16	Not for me	90
17	Station wagon	78
18	Is unimportant	72
19	Chevrolet	64
20	Informal	58
21	Squirrel	49
22	Commonplace	44
23	Cheap	36
24	Low quality	31
25	In bad taste	31
26	Picnic	31
27	Bad	20
28	Unattractive	19
Total		8,348

ASSOCIATION TEST: Parliament Chevron-Crest Package
Without Identity

Sample: 604 Cigarette Smokers   *December 5, 1955*

ANALYSIS

This test, of the Parliament Chevron-Crest Package without identity, shows that the design is as effective without the Parliament identity as it is with the identity (previously tested).

The *for me* association is stronger when the package does not have the Parliament identity. I believe we are safe in assuming that the name being associated with high price brings the *for me* rating down. However, it is not brought down very much.

The two tests, with and without identity, show clearly that this is a most effective cigarette package design.

Percentage of Individuals

Words	301 Men	303 Women	604 Total
Good	88	94	91
Bad	12	6	9
Strong	26	22	24
Mild	70	77	74
Masculine	51	45	48
Feminine	50	58	54
High quality	87	94	91
Low quality	13	5	9
Ordinary	20	15	18
Distinctive	80	85	82
Smart	86	95	90
Commonplace	14	5	9
Bright	95	96	96
Dull	5	4	4
Attractive	92	96	94
Unattractive	8	4	6
Mediocre	27	14	20
Outstanding	73	86	79
Original	89	91	90
Old-fashioned	11	8	9
Undesirable	13	5	9
Desirable	87	95	91
Costly	93	92	93
Cheap	6	8	7
Appealing	89	96	93
Unappealing	10	3	7
Tasteful	55	76	66
Flashy	45	23	34
Confused	11	9	10
Clean	89	91	90
For me	70	82	76
Not for me	30	17	23

OCULAR MEASUREMENTS: Three Parliament Ads

August 3, 1964

ANALYSIS

Of the three ads, Ad No. 1 is only fair in eye flow because there is hesitation and the illustrations to the left of the Parliament package get no attention.

Ad No. 2 is only fair in eye flow because there is hesitation and the illustrations to the left of the Parliament package get no attention.

Ad No. 3 is excellent in eye flow because the three major points—the package, the filter and bold copy—on the ad get attention.

	Rating
Ad No. 1	
After considerable hesitation, eyes fell on Parliament package at lower right, moved up to *Parliament Takes An Extra Step And Adds Activated Charcoal* and left ad.	C (Fair)
Ad No. 2	
After considerable hesitation, eyes fell on Parliament package at lower right, moved up to *Now Parliament Takes An Extra Step And Adds Activated Charcoal* and left ad.	C (Fair)
Ad No. 3	
Eyes fell on Parliament package at lower right, moved to cigarette filter with "V," up to *Now Parliament Takes An Extra Step And Adds Activated Charcoal* and left ad.	A (Excellent)

OCULAR MEASUREMENTS: Alpine Gold Cigarette Package

June 1, 1966

ANALYSIS

Visibility of the package as a whole is good.
Readability of *Alpine* is fairly good.
Eye flow and attention-holding are excellent.

Ocular Measurements	Rating
Visibility	81
Readability—Alpine	76
Eye Movement—Eyes fell on *Alpine* and symbol, moved up to red tab and left package. Attention was held on *Alpine* and symbol.	A (Excellent)

7

CONSOWELD CORPORATION

SINCE 1954, LCA–CRI has conducted studies of Consoweld literature—catalog pages, booklets and ads, and has carried out a testing program of new patterns for plastic laminates for the kitchen, dinette tables, etc.

A new pattern that rates as high as the best-selling pattern in association and preference was put into the line. The reports reproduced here, in part, are representative of the research for Consoweld.

OCULAR MEASUREMENTS: Catalog–Consoweld 6

November 26, 1956

ANALYSIS

COVER: The cover is very effective. It guides the eyes smoothly.

The eye-movement test does not show any negative element. However, I suggest centering the Consoweld trade name and trademark at the bottom of the cover.

DOUBLE SPREAD: There is an element of hesitation. However, the eyes move smoothly across both pages. The hesitation may not be with the printed two-page spread.

BACK: The illustration at right is too strong for the one at left. The left side should always have the stronger illustration and more vibrant color.

Rarely does a person move his eyes from right to left. The hesitation is caused by the illustration at the right being stronger than the one at the left.

Cover

    Eye Movement—Eyes fell on head of figure, moved to apple, to little girl, moved across yellow counter to two half apples, to object on counter at right, to red pan on wall, to picture frame at right and left page.

Rating

A (Excellent)

Double Spread

    Eye Movement—After some hesitation, eyes fell on head of girl, moved to blue bowl near sink, back to girl's hair, to red pot on blue counter, to fruit, to point of counter, on right page, to yellow table on illustration to the right, to pink object on cabinet of lower right illustration, to bottom left corner of illustration, to right and left page.

B (Good)

Back

    Eye Movement—After some hesitation, eyes fell on yellow counter at right, moved to girl's head, after some effort moved back to yellow counter, then to pink wall, to standing girl on left side and left page.

C (Fair)

OCULAR MEASUREMENTS: Catalog—Consoweld 10

November 26, 1956

ANALYSIS

FRONT OF PAGE: The illustration demands effort. It lacks a point of focus. If figure stands out in actual photo, it will "split" the illustration. The reader will have a tendency to move to the right. We don't know whether there is enough interest in the actual photo to pull the eyes back to the left.

BACK OF PAGE: The flow is good. It may be excellent after the copy is in position on the printed page. The yellow above the green Consoweld on the lower illustration is too strong. It should be almost white or gray.

Front of Page Rating

Eye Movement—Eyes had difficulty in focusing at any one point. D (Poor)

Back of Page

Eye Movement—Eyes fell on wall of upper left illustration, moved to drapery tieback, door in upper right illustration, across yellow wall in lower right illustration and left page. B (Good)

OCULAR MEASUREMENTS: Three Consoweld Ads

February 21, 1964

ANALYSIS

CONSOWELD AD: 1
The layout is excellent.

CONSOWELD AD: 2
The layout is poor because it lacks a point of focus.

CONSOWELD AD: 3
This layout is also poor because it lacks a point of focus.

RECOMMENDATIONS

The larger layout, Consoweld Ad 3, I think can be saved by using some kind of an illustration at the left, as indicated on the tissue.

Consoweld Ad 1 Rating

Eye Movement—Eyes fell on figure in uniform, moved to other man, to illustration on table, to chips below, to Consoweld symbol, up to *have you explored Consoweld's new world of color* and left ad. A (Excellent)

Consoweld Ad 2

Eye Movement—Eyes could not focus at any point. D (Poor)

Consoweld Ad 3

Eye Movement—Eyes could not focus at any point. D (Poor)

ASSOCIATION TEST: Four Consoweld Patterns
#606 vs. #607 vs. #605 vs. #608

Sample: 300 Consumers   *May 23, 1966*

ANALYSIS

Tan Travertine has greater consumer acceptance than Gray Royale and Gray Burl.

Off-White Whisper has 79 percent favorable associations, Tan Travertine 71 percent, Gray Royale 38 percent, and Gray Burl 18 percent.

The total number of favorable responses (favorable impact) is 387 for Off-White Whisper, 250 for Tan Travertine, 173 for Gray Royale, and 90 for Gray Burl.

Off-White Whisper rates highest with each of the favorable attitude terms and Tan Travertine is second highest.

For some specific uses Tan Travertine rates very high. It rates higher with "coffee table tops" than does any of the other three patterns. It also has a large number of associations with "kitchen counters" and "dinette table tops."

The test results show that Tan Travertine has considerably more acceptance than either Gray Royale or Gray Burl. Since these test results have been confirmed with a sample of an additional 100 respondents, it is advisable to add Tan Travertine to the line.

Percentage of Favorable and Unfavorable Associations

	#606 Tan Travertine	#607 Gray Royale	#605 Off-White Whisper	#608 Gray Burl
Favorable	71	38	79	18
Unfavorable	29	62	21	82

ASSOCIATION TEST: Four Consoweld Patterns

Number of Associations

Favorable	#606 Tan Travertine	#607 Gray Royale	#605 Off-White Whisper	#608 Gray Burl
High quality	89	61	121	29
Attractive	80	67	118	35
For me	81	45	148	26
Total	250	173	387	90
Unfavorable				
Low quality	26	98	32	144
Unattractive	36	94	29	141
Not for me	39	87	42	132
Total	101	279	103	417
Unclassified				
Kitchen wainscoting	62	66	132	40
Kitchen counters	90	50	111	49
Dinette table tops	88	65	116	31
Coffee table tops	122	58	80	39
Vanity tops	74	73	117	36
Bathroom walls	70	35	161	34
Grand total	857	799	1,207	736

ASSOCIATION TEST: Four Backsplash Designs
#611 vs. #610 vs. #609 vs. #612

Sample: 400 Consumers　　　　　　　　　　　*June 1, 1966*

ANALYSIS

Lamplighter and Medallion have considerably more consumer acceptance than Colonial and Spice.

Lamplighter has 71 percent favorable associations, Medallion 71 percent, Spice 50 percent, and Colonial 26 percent.

The total number of favorable responses (favorable impact) is 1,156 for Lamplighter, 1,129 for Medallion, 699 for Colonial, and 613 for Spice.

Lamplighter and Medallion rate higher than Colonial and Spice with each of the favorable attitude terms.

Lamplighter is most frequently considered "for period kitchen."

Lamplighter, Medallion, and Spice all rate about equally high with "for contemporary kitchen."

Colonial rates highest with "for modern kitchen," but rates very low in percentage of favorable associations.

The results show that Lamplighter and Medallion have greater consumer acceptance than Colonial or Spice.

The second set of 200 responses confirms the results of the first 200 responses. This confirmation indicates that Colonial and Spice should not be put into the line.

Percentage of Favorable and Unfavorable Associations

	#611 Colonial	#610 Lamplighter	#609 Medallion	#612 Spice
Favorable	26	71	71	50
Unfavorable	74	29	29	50

ASSOCIATION TEST: Four Backsplash Designs

Number of Associations

Favorable	#611 Colonial	#610 Lamplighter	#609 Medallion	#612 Spice
Good	85	129	119	67
High quality	74	133	128	65
Appealing	82	129	123	66
Attractive	83	117	125	75
Pleasing	67	134	128	70
Desirable	80	117	133	70
High class	75	123	129	71
Expensive	74	141	122	63
For me	79	133	122	66
Total	**699**	**1,156**	**1,129**	**613**
Unfavorable				
Bad	220	57	54	69
Low quality	209	49	57	85
Unappealing	222	54	49	75
Unattractive	221	56	49	73
Not pleasing	235	43	48	72
Undesirable	222	59	48	70
Low class	242	41	54	61
Cheap	222	58	53	65
Not for me	246	59	46	49
Total	**2,039**	**476**	**458**	**619**
Unclassified				
For modern kitchen	188	42	50	120
For contemporary kitchen	46	120	121	111
For period kitchen	46	143	112	99
Grand total	**3,018**	**1,937**	**1,870**	**1,562**

8

THE HIRES COMPANY

HOW HIRES TOOK THE GAMBLE OUT OF NEW PACKAGE CHANGE

From the *W/S Review*, April, 1965

"What's in a package? A lot of time-consuming research, market analysis and testing, design problems, motivational research studies, more time and money, and ultimately the hope that the finished package will help to sell more of the product it represents. Packaging design changes are becoming more costly all the time. Why Hires Root Beer decided to change its package and trademark is the basis for this story.

"Marketing conditions and consumer responses change. This marketing principle formed the basis for the Hires Division of Beverages International Inc. decision to change the packaging and trademark of Hires Root Beer. Proper timing was another factor which played an important part in the decision to build into the product more appeal at the point of purchase.

"Hires Vice President, Frank S. O'Donnell, recalls that when Beverages International Inc. purchased Hires Root Beer about two and a half years ago, 'We were interested in studying all phases of marketing.'

" 'Alert management is forced to meet changing consumer reactions to its products. Because of this we are constantly on the lookout for new ways and means to improve our competitive position in the soft drink field. Hires had established itself as the leading root beer for nearly ninety years, but we needed to learn more about consumer preferences. In addition, we wanted to know what had been done with Hires by previous owners and what could be done in the future to increase consumption and gain greater shelf movement,' said Frank O'Donnell.

"Part of the Hires investigation led to an analysis of the product and the package. At this point, it was felt that management needed guidance from an unbiased source. Hires set about to take advantage of available information in the behavioral sciences, namely psychology and motivational research. It was felt that using scientific methods to determine consumer motivation might lead to additional sales.

"Hires was fortunate to have in nearby Chicago the advice, guidance, and previous research findings of Louis Cheskin Associates, who with twenty years' experience in marketing research had demonstrated that packaging is a vital marketing factor. According to Louis Cheskin, consumers think they buy only the product, but in reality they are influenced more often than they realize by the package. However, when consumers are confronted in a direct interview, they will say that the product inside the package is the only thing which motivates their choice.

" 'Our research has disclosed,' said Cheskin, 'that the consumer is unconsciously motivated by the package and/or the advertisement.' He explained that when the consumer is confronted with two packages, each containing the identical product, she will base her opinion and choice of product upon the package itself.

"This underlying basis for the consumer's choice can be revealed through what Cheskin labeled 'controlled motivational research,' wherein the consumer will unwittingly reveal a transfer of the sensation she gets from the package to the product inside. It was learned that such phenomena, known as 'sensation transference,' can be measured under a series of carefully controlled tests.

"Hires decided to test the package it was using at the time, and submitted its carton to a series of 'ocular measurement tests.' The tests are designed to measure the eye flow and movement over a package and to test its attention-holding ability. In these tests, Cheskin Associates determined that the 'visibility of the carton as a whole,' that the 'readability of the Hires trademark,' and that the 'attention-holding powers' of the carton indicated that Hires consider redesigning the package for greater eye-appeal and attention-getting powers.

" 'Because of their former success in the soft drink packaging design field, we employed Charles Akers & Associates, Chicago package design firm,' said Frank O'Donnell. Akers produced three prototypes, which were then put through the same tests to determine their display effectiveness as compared with the old carton design. Two of the new prototypes yielded highly favorable ratings over the old carton design. Both were very much the same, the sole exception being the addition of a third color in the dot of the 'I' in Hires. The 'visibility of the carton as a whole' rated a 'very good,' the 'readability of the trademark' improved to a 'very good,' and it was determined that the 'eye-movement and attention-holding powers' were 'excellent.'

"Based upon the results of these preliminary studies, Hires management decided to compare responses between the old and one of the new designs. The three-color new carton was chosen to be compared with the old Hires carton because it was found to have greater motivational appeal than any of the other three prototypes.

"A series of 'association' and 'preference' tests were outlined by Cheskin. In the association tests, respondents were given the opportunity to associate specific terms with the product through word association, when comparing the two cartons. Typical phrases which respondents could select through word association were: 'higher quality' or 'lower quality,' 'more refreshing' or 'less refreshing,' 'more expensive ingredients' or 'less expensive ingredients.' (It should be noted that both cartons contained the identical product.)

"In the consumer preference tests, respondents were given the opportunity to choose which of the two packages they preferred. In-depth surveys were conducted with a segment of housewives in Chicago and Philadelphia. The sample segment was large enough, according to Cheskin, to predict with more than 92 percent accuracy.

"Through 'favorable association,' an attitude on the part of the respondent was correlated, while in the 'consumer preference' phase of the study, the respondent revealed her actual choice—a choice in which a high degree of self-interest is involved.

"The results of these tests indicated that the newly created package communicated to the consumer that Hires Root Beer in the proposed carton design rated very high in favorable associations and in preference, far greater than the carton then in use.

"The new carton, which is designed with a striking wood-grained effect, symbolic of the Hires Root Beer barrel, carries a new trademark with a curving arch above and below the product name. The curves were utilized to be symbolic of a smile. Other colors besides the dark brown shades of the carton, are orange, white, and blue-green. New crowns have been designed and a similar logo has been designed for the Hires bottles to help boost sales.

"Louis Cheskin said that the 'Hires Root Beer repackaging program is an excellent example of the power of packaging through controlled motivational research, showing clearly that Hires Root Beer in the new package has a much greater consumer acceptance than Hires in the present carton.' He predicted that the new carton would yield 'from 50 to 75 percent increase in sales if all other marketing factors remain about the same, or if other sales aspects were at least as good.'

"The new package was introduced into a test market in Tucson, Arizona. Results of the test revealed that sales rose above the predicted increase. As a result of this thorough investigation by Hires, Vice President Frank O'Donnell is enthusiastic over the future of the product. New enthusiasm has been injected into the bottler selling force."

ASSOCIATION TEST: Hires Root Beer Six-Packs— Present Carton vs. Carton Design 1:4

Sample: 400 Consumers   *January 3, 1964*

ANALYSIS

The root beer in Carton Design 1:4 has much greater consumer acceptance than the root beer in the Present Carton.

In Chicago, Carton Design 1:4 has 72 percent favorable associations and 76 percent preference. The Present Carton has 28 percent favorable associations and 24 percent preference.

In Philadelphia, Carton Design 1:4 has 60 percent favorable associations and 60 percent preference. The Present Carton has 41 percent favorable associations and 40 percent preference.

The root beer in Carton Design 1:4 has a larger number of associations with each of the favorable attitude terms than does the root beer in the Present Carton.

The root beer in Carton Design 1:4 has the larger number of associations with "dry," "light," "lower sugar content," "modern," and "for younger people." The root beer in the Present Carton has the larger number of associations with "sweet," "heavy," "higher sugar content," "old-fashioned," and "for older people."

The results of the test show clearly that Carton Design 1:4 is a far more effective package than the Present Carton.

SUMMARY TABLE

Chicago—Total	Present Carton	Carton Design 1:4
Favorable associations	28%	72%
Preference	24%	76%
Men		
Favorable associations	27%	73%
Preference	25%	75%
Women		
Favorable associations	29%	71%
Preference	23%	77%
Philadelphia—Total		
Favorable associations	41%	60%
Preference	40%	60%
Men		
Favorable associations	39%	61%
Preference	37%	63%
Women		
Favorable associations	44%	58%
Preference	43%	57%

9

BLUE STAR FOODS

BLUE STAR BASED MARKETING PROGRAM
ON PACKAGE IMPROVEMENT

The following case history illustrates how a marketer continued to improve his package and used it as a basis for building a very successful business.

"Fairmont Foods Company of Omaha announced today that it will, through an exchange of common stock, acquire 100 percent control of Blue Star Foods, Inc., Rockford, Illinois. Blue Star is one of the leading manufacturers and distributors of potato chips in its trade area, which is concentrated in the northern half of Illinois. Distribution also covers portions of Iowa, Wisconsin, and Minnesota.

"Plans are now being formulated to expand the Rockford product line with new and improved snack items being developed in Fairmont's research laboratory in Omaha.

"There will be no changes in operating personnel, administrative policies, trade names or customer relations."

The above three paragraphs appeared in the press, July, 1963.

Harry T. McNamara was vice president and sales manager. I met Harry McNamara in August, 1955. He brought a package to me for testing. There was an immediate understanding between us and we had confidence in each other.

The following is from the report on his package:

A star is an excellent marketing device. It is an attention-getter. The star is an image that has high preference (appeal) and strong retention in the memory. We don't know exactly the degree of favorable associations it has, but we know that it has no unfavorable associations.

The deep blue and orange-red are high-preference colors that are appropriate for potato chips. The deep blue is complementary to the color of the potato chips. The orange-red is warm and it rates high in association with foods.

In spite of the very effective brand-identifying imagery and the right colors, the package has a visibility rating of only 74, a brand-name readability of 76, and the eye-movement test shows that the package does not hold attention.

This package can be made into an effective marketing tool without having its identity changed. I recommend that the package be redesigned with the following elements given consideration:

1. Eliminate the small stars. They are hard on the eyes. They take attention away from the large brand-identifying star.

2. Enlarge the circle and star containing the brand name to emphasize brand identity.

3. Enlarge and simplify the lettering of *Blue Star* to increase readability.

4. Use red instead of white at the top and at the bottom of the bag to increase visibility of the package as a whole.

5. Keep the space in the circle around the star clear white so that the star will have stronger visibility.

6. Make *Potato Chips* in one line and blue instead of red. Blue, being a complementary color to the potato chips, will be more readable and it will make the potato chips stand out more.

Send the new design to Color Research Institute for ocular measurements—visibility, readability, and eye-movement tests.

After about two months of creative work, McNamara sent in three new designs for testing.

One package design rated excellent in visibility from the shelf (94), very good in readability of brand name *Blue Star* (87), and excellent in eye flow and attention-holding. This design was put into a field test—a controlled association test with a sample of 400 consumers in two geographic areas.

Test results: The old package rated 37 percent in favorable associations and the new one 65 percent. The potato chips in the old package had 33 percent declared preference, and in the new package 67 percent.

In my analysis I brought out that a great increase in sales can be generated by the new package alone, with all other marketing factors remaining the same. I added that this package can, however, serve as the basis for a dynamic marketing program. McNamara said to me later that a dynamic marketing program is what he had in mind.

What have been the marketing results? The following shows the growth in sales since the new package was introduced:

YEAR	SALES
1955 (base year)	100%
1956 (3 months)	117%
1957 (first full year of new package)	214%
1958	275%
1959	392%
1960	453%
1961 (package again improved)	771%
1962	906%
1963 (6 months)	1,078%

A new Blue Star Foods plant was built in 1960. It provides 50,000 square feet of floor space.

Fairmont Foods Company was impressed. This is a success story. It is the story of management that is scientifically minded and consumer-oriented. It is the story of marketing men who are up-to-date and alert to the changes in the American scene and who know how to combine all the necessary elements for a marketing success.

ASSOCIATION TESTS: **Blue Star Potato Chip Bag**

Sample: 401 Consumers *April 18, 1957*

TEST A: Present Package vs. New Design
(10-cent size)

TEST B: Present Package vs. New Design (without window)
(39-cent size)

ANALYSIS

In the 10-cent size the New Design receives 66 percent favorable associations and the Present Package 42 percent.

In the 39-cent size the Present Package receives 66 percent favorable associations and the New Design (without window) 35 percent.

Evidently the New Design is effective with the window but not without it.

**Percentage of Total Favorable and
Total Unfavorable Associations**

10¢ Size Bags	Present Package	New Design
Total favorable	42	66
Total unfavorable	58	34

**Percentage of Total Favorable and
Total Unfavorable Associations**

39¢ Size Bags	Present Package	New Design (without window)
Total favorable	66	35
Total unfavorable	34	65

TEST A: Present Package vs. New Design
(10-cent size)

Number of Associations

Words	Present Package	New Design
Favorable		
Good	85	116
High quality	70	126
Attractive	72	127
Appealing	74	126
Desirable	82	116
Distinctive	56	136
Fresh	72	119
For me	75	120
Total	586	986
Unfavorable		
Bad	87	64
Low quality	105	65
Unattractive	107	58
Unappealing	106	67
Undesirable	93	68
Ordinary	124	57
Stale	87	61
Not for me	98	67
Total	807	507
Grand total	1,393	1,493

TEST B: Present Package vs. New Design (without window) (39-cent size)

Number of Associations

Words	Present Package	New Design (without window)
Favorable		
Good	141	59
High quality	135	64
Attractive	128	73
Appealing	139	59
Desirable	138	62
Distinctive	96	104
Fresh	130	69
For me	134	65
Total	1,041	555
Unfavorable		
Bad	57	140
Low quality	62	133
Unattractive	70	124
Unappealing	57	140
Undesirable	60	134
Ordinary	113	84
Stale	66	128
Not for me	62	133
Total	547	1,016
Grand total	1,588	1,571

ASSOCIATION TEST: Consumer Attitudes toward
Five Potato Chip Pictorials that Differ in Color

Sample: 200 Consumers   *March 10, 1964*

ANALYSIS

The pictorials with Color C and Color E rate much higher than any of the other pictorials in percentage of favorable associations, in declared preference ("for me") and in favorable impact (total number of favorable associations).

The potato chips in pictorials C and E both rate about equally high with each of the favorable attitude terms. However, Color E has a larger number of associations with "highest calories" than does Color C.

The pictorial with Color D rates high in percentage of favorable associations and in preference, but not as high as the pictorials with Color C and Color E.

The pictorials with Color A and Color B are completely lacking in effectiveness.

Color A has   0% favorable associations and   0% declared preference.
Color B has   5% favorable associations and   0% declared preference.
Color C has 91% favorable associations and 38% declared preference.
Color D has 84% favorable associations and 23% declared preference.
Color E has 92% favorable associations and 37% declared preference.

The results of the test show clearly that the pictorial with Color C is the most effective of the five pictorials.

Because Color E rates higher than Color C in association with "calories" it is less desirable.

10

G. D. SEARLE

THE ANALYSIS of this test is reproduced here because several "experts" could not see any significant difference between the two containers. The research shows that the new container greatly increased consumer acceptance of the product.

ASSOCIATION TEST: Searle Metamucil
Present Container vs. Proposed Container

Sample: 400 Respondents   *August 10, 1965*

ANALYSIS

The Proposed Container has far more consumer acceptance than the Present Container.

FLORIDA:
The vegetable powder in the Proposed Container has 82 percent favorable associations; that in the Present Container 18 percent.
The preference is 87 percent for the powder in the Proposed Container and 13 percent for the powder in the Present Container.
The powder in the Proposed Container rates much higher than that in the Present Container with each of the favorable attitude terms except "contains more."
In the Proposed Container, the price of the powder is most frequently considered $2.95. In the Present Container, the price of the powder is most frequently considered $2.45.

CALIFORNIA:
The vegetable powder in the Proposed Container has 69 percent favorable associations; that in the Present Container 31 percent.

The preference is 76 percent for the powder in the Proposed Container and 24 percent for the powder in the Present Container.

The powder in the Proposed Container rates much higher than that in the Present Container with each of the favorable attitude terms except "contains more."

In the Proposed Container, the powder is more frequently associated with $2.95 and $3.45 than with any of the other prices. In the Present Container, the price of the powder is most frequently considered $2.95.

CONCLUSION

The test results in both areas show clearly that the Proposed Container is much more effective than the Present Container.

11

LAVOPTIK COMPANY

THIS COMPANY is included in this book to show how a small company makes use of research to determine the effectiveness of proposed package designs and advertising themes.

OCULAR MEASUREMENTS: Lavoptik Eye Lotion Carton (New Design)

August 31, 1961

ANALYSIS

Visibility of the package as a whole is very good.
Readability of *Lavoptik* on carton is good and on bottle is fairly good. (It was very poor on the other bottle.)
Eye flow and attention-holding are excellent.

Ocular Measurements	Rating
Visibility	85
Readability—Lavoptik (carton)	80
—Lavoptik (bottle)	72
Eye Movement—Eyes fell on *Lavoptik* at bottom of carton, moved to *Eye Lotion* at right, to *Lavoptik* on bottle, up to *Free!* at upper left, moved to right and left package. Attention was held at each point.	A (Excellent)

ASSOCIATION TEST: Five Proposed Marketing Themes for Lavoptik

Sample: 400 Women   *June 25, 1963*

ANALYSIS

The results of the test show clearly that Theme No. 4 ("Soothes and relieves irritated eye misery") is by far the most effective of the five themes in the test.

Theme No. 4 has the highest percentage of favorable associations and the highest percentage of preference, both in urban and suburban Chicago.

Theme No. 4 has the greatest favorable impact (total number of favorable associations) and the least unfavorable impact.

This test shows clearly that Theme No. 4 will make the greatest contribution to Lavoptik.

Percentage of Favorable and Unfavorable Associations

	Theme No. 1	Theme No. 2	Theme No. 3	Theme No. 4	Theme No. 5
Favorable	47	20	44	85	26
Unfavorable	53	80	56	15	74

Preference

	Number	Percent
Theme No. 1	25	12
Theme No. 2	7	3
Theme No. 3	40	24
Theme No. 4	97	48
Theme No. 5	23	11

12

T. EATON COMPANY

THE FOLLOWING REPORTS SHOW how eye-movement tests are used for determining how consumers look at catalog pages—which elements or articles on the page get and hold attention and which do not.

OCULAR MEASUREMENTS: Eaton's Summer Sale Catalog Cover

April 21, 1966

ANALYSIS

CATALOG COVER A is only fair because there is considerable hesitation and the space at the bottom left of the page gets no attention.

CATALOG COVER B has good eye flow but not excellent because the bottom left of the page gets no attention.

CATALOG COVER C is good but not excellent because the bottom left of the page gets no attention.

CATALOG COVER D is poor because there is considerable hesitation and the lower half of the page gets no attention.

RECOMMENDATION

Cover B and Cover C could be improved considerably by moving the copy at the right to the left and the detailed copy on the left to the right.

Cover A: **Rating**

    Eye Movement—After considerable hesitation, eyes fell on   C (Fair)
        EATON'S, moved to *Summer Sale Extra, to*
        radio illustration, to *69.00* and left page.

Cover B:

    Eye Movement—Eyes fell on *EATON'S,* moved to *Summer Sale*   B (Good)
        Extra, to radio illustration, to *69.00* and left
        page.

Cover C:

    Eye Movement—Eyes fell on *EATON'S,* moved to *Summer Sale*   B (Good)
        Extra, to radio illustration, to *69.00* and left
        page.

Cover D:

    Eye Movement—After considerable hesitation, eyes fell on   D (Poor)
        EXTRA, moved up to *SUMMER SALE EATON'S*
        and left page.

NOW YOU KNOW
THE SECRETS OF
MARKETING SUCCESS

IF YOU HAVE READ this book from the beginning to the end, you are a searcher for new methods to achieve success.

The fact that you were able to read it indicates that you have a frame of reference that the contents of this book did not contradict or that you have an open mind and are aware that changing conditions in our society and, therefore, in business make a new frame of reference necessary.

One who is not problem-directed cannot read this book. You have read it. Therefore, you can proceed to solve problems in the light of the new facts, with the advantage of a frame of reference that is applicable to present-day problems in business—the problems of marketing products that fulfill psychological needs or wants.

If you are a marketer of consumer products, you will not waste precious time and great sums of money on test markets until you have ascertained through controlled, structured motivation research that each component of your marketing program is effective. You will predetermine the consumer acceptance of the product and the communicating and motivating power of the package—brand symbol, color, and the advertising—marketing theme, graphics, etc.

If you are in the marketing research field you will organize

your testing procedures with the best controls you can develop for keeping the tests on an unconscious level. You will
design your tests so that they will reveal how effective the
marketing tool is in communicating about the product and in
motivating consumers, not how it rates as a work of art.

You know now, if you did not know before, that to be able
to produce research results on which management can make
marketing decisions you must first of all fully understand
"sensation transference" and you must implement controls so
that the respondent's ego does not get involved in the research situation.

By testing all of the marketing elements of a marketing
program—package and advertising—on an unconscious level
with reliable controls, you will yourself be in a position to
make marketing predictions on share of market.

If you are a marketing man, now that you have read this
book and have given some thought to the principles and
the facts presented in it, you are aware that in our day most
products are designed to satisfy psychological needs or wants,
not merely biological necessities.

You now are aware that we must use psychological means
for selling psychologically meaningful commodities. And in
order to determine whether your product is psychologically
satisfying, you must use marketing research techniques that
reveal consumers' true attitudes and feelings. Now you know
that polling or direct interviewing cannot disclose feelings
about psychologically significant, but biologically, practically,
or functionally insignificant factors. Only motivation research
can reveal the actual attitudes and feelings of consumers
about psychologically significant elements.

I wanted to include in this book more of my clients. Space
did not permit discussion of the very interesting program of
changing the entire catalog of the Ortho-Vent Shoe Company
and the research project that led to the introduction of a new
brand of shoes—Stuart McGuire. This company of which
Cabell Brand is President and very active director is unique in

its operation. And I had to leave out some brand image and corporate image studies and studies of "images" of political candidates. But, I think, I have achieved the objective of this book.

Now you know the secrets of marketing success.

GLOSSARY

Brand image

The consumer's concept of the brand; what consumers believe about the brand; the favorable and/or unfavorable connotations of the brand.

Consumer sample

A representative number of consumers, as a group representing users of cake-mixes, cough medicine, or candy.

Corporate image

The public's concept of the corporation; what the public thinks of the corporation; the favorable and/or unfavorable aspects of the company; how people feel about the company; attitudes toward the company.

Defense mechanisms

Self-protective actions or statements; expressions for covering up true feelings; defensive measures.

Ego involvement

Involvement with the ego or self; a person reacting on the basis of his ego, not objectively on the basis of facts; defensive.

Indirect approach

An interviewer presenting a problem indirectly, not straight to the point, and getting a respondent's true attitude without his knowing that he is revealing his feelings.

Involuntary reactions

Reactions that are not intended; reactions that are not consciously controlled, such as being attracted by an object that stands out or a package in the supermarket that draws attention.

Motivation research

The type of research that seeks to learn what motivates consumers in making choices; research that reveals which of a number of units—names, symbols, packages, headlines, or ads—has greatest appeal to consumers or is most motivating.

Psychological satisfactions

Things that are not essential for sustaining life; things that are satisfying or pleasing, such as fashionable clothes, design, cake, but are not necessary for biological survival.

Sensation transference

Transferring the sensation from one thing to another, as from the package to the product it contains; judging a book by its cover or a person by his attire.

Subjectivity

Considering all things on the basis of personal feelings; purely personal reaction.

Subliminal

Below the threshold of consciousness; subconscious.

Symbolism

Representing things by symbols; symbolic meaning or character.

Unconscious

Not aware; devoid of awareness; a package or ad having an effect on a person, without his being aware of the effect.

Unconscious level testing

Testing on a level of unawareness; a test in which an interview is conducted without the respondent being aware specifically what the interviewer wants to know; a test in which respondents express their feelings and reveal their attitudes without realizing that they are reacting.

INDEX